CHRISTMAS 97.

Yo DAD,

HAVE A LOVELY CHRISTMAS.
LOTS OF LOVE,
CAOIMHE xxx

# The Grey Area

## Sean
## Hughes

PAVILION

First published in Great Britain in 1996 by
Pavilion Books Limited
26 Upper Ground
London SE1 9PD

First published in hardback in 1995

Designed by Cole design unit

Jacket photograph by Nic Barlow

A CIP catalogue record for this book is available from the British Library

ISBN 1-85793-868-2

Phototypeset in 10/13 pt Meridien with Frutiger 55 by
Textype Typesetters, Cambridge
Printed and bound in Great Britain by Cox & Wyman Ltd, Reading

2 4 6 8 10 9 7 5 3 1

This book may be ordered by post direct from the publisher. Please contact
the Marketing Department. But try your bookshop first.

To all those who have the choice and yet
choose not to watch daytime television but especially to
H and R and M and D and C
and somebody whose identity has to be kept secret
who I shall call Mr X
suffice to say he has done maverick work forwarding
the black movement with an equally special thanks to
A. B. E. F. G. I. J. K. L. N. O. P. Q. S. T. U. V. W. Y and Z.

# Contents

# Contents

# Foreword

I feel I ought to explain what I mean by The Grey Area, not an exact explanation because I'm a firm believer in letting people reach their own conclusions. The title came after the book was completed. It wasn't my starting point but on re-reading the various pieces the expression kept cropping up. A rather dour title for a book, I know, and of course people have tried to wean me away from using it. This is understandable, their argument being that the phrase is loaded with negative connotations. But I have made the decision to remain true to myself and to stay in line with the effect this collection is trying to provoke. It is certainly not a case of going against the grain just for the sake of it, it comes more from scratching at the surface and finding all not seeming as expected. This excited me and has led me to question rather than accept.

To me this is an ongoing search as I fear that the continual thought patterns pressed upon us by our society breed association not individual thought. We are told what to expect from our lives leaving subcultures to sink into smaller subcultures. The mass media, although outwardly appearing to span various spectrums, is silted and stuck because it is coming from the same starting point. The only development allowed is to push towards repetition. Our sparkling society is moved by trends and hype alone. The individual is not to blame. Within the extreme parameters of our civilization we are only allowed an acceptable level of thought. All else is outlawed or pushed underground. One man's limitations are another one's springboard. As a race we love to quote the maxims but never act upon them. Synthetic arguments will constantly collide on top of each other stating 'this is what the public wants' rather than is given. The opinion polls are all very well but maybe we are being asked the wrong questions.

The Grey Area is the bridge between everything. No answers, just more interesting questions. This area can be split into more sub-groups ad infinitum. It caters for those who fear they are not being catered for. There are never any absolute truths and there never can be. This comes from the depressing knowledge that we can never be as one. This sticks in the mind as a theory which seems blatantly obvious and like most, is never really taken on board. Certain do-gooders (who we need) see this problem as one of race and religion but isn't it only an evolving pattern? Looking back over earth's short existence, humans have always grouped together protecting their own circles while dismissing the rest.

Today it is becoming impossible to even group. The family is dead as people cower in their own slime frightened to see it as the pretence it is. And why is this so? The main reason has to be because we have been given this time-table of civilized society and we don't really want to question something so structured. Instead we allow ourselves to become these so-called members of civilized society: birth, school, work, death with a little interaction thrown in. And why not? There seems to be no other option or the option there is is a terrifying one. We end up spending our lives in little pigeon-holes where only a few dimensions of our personality are allowed to flourish. The rest of our psyche is put under the big banner of frustration giving us, among other things, negative feelings. Rather than seeing this through, we block and push these thoughts away as far as they will go. Unfortunately such thoughts don't go away, they re-surface from time to time and this is what we deem the human condition.

This work is composed of asking questions about questions we don't bother to ask and in doing so hopefully keeping in touch to redefine for the times we live in. This is our responsibility after all. It is not a structured collection or a soap-boxed rant, it is basically what I have been thinking about for the last two years. The Grey Area is a beautiful place to be. A supposed mixture of black (the dark side) and white (purity) and yet our dictionary definition states: dull, dismal, neutral, anonymous, an area between two extremes. To the main it is seen as a situation to which there are no clear-cut distinctions. To me there is no place more extreme. I am aware there can be no dogma as each's grey area differs from the next depending on where the black and white are located. Come into The Grey Area, the balance of life lies here. O, and there's a few jokes along the way as well.

There are more of us a-coming
There are more like me
Messed up, messed up
With nothing to lose

*most reverend Julian Cope*

# The Grey Area

# Me, Again

Don't let me near that gun
The deafness of the left-hander
Won't ponder the explosion
Knocking on the door
It won't open
And yet I am heard
And is it really a comfort to know
There are others in this predicament
Yes we can all shrug our shoulders
In unison
Then feel as stupid as we're supposed to
We call their bluff
And the door is opened
But we refuse to leave

# Extracts from my Autobiography

With only five hundred odd shopping days left before Christmas after next, you are probably looking for stocking fillers. Luckily this is the time publishers dump every egghead's self-indulgent rendition of their life on to the bookshelf, yes it's autobiography time. The books where people arrogantly try to make sense of their lives for us. We get to read about their childhood foibles, junkets of their wild youth and the mannered approach to middle age. Of course the juicy bits are hidden away in the hazy memory section of the psyche. The reason for publishing such daubings being that the book will act as a prism into their confession box. I, for one, don't want to hear about their ruttings, and I am sure they don't need our forgiveness. And why all the padding? Terry Venables talks us through his mother's childhood. I don't even want to know about my own mother's childhood. Autobiographies should be brought out in pamphlet form. Let's just cut to the chase.

George Best – good footballer, drank a lot. Do we need to know any more?
Seb Coe – ran for his country, neat hair, became a pal of John Major.
Sean Hughes – crap at football, ran in the country, drank a lot, messy hair, hates fascists.

I have decided never to write an autobiography, but instead here is my official authorised pamphlet. I've called it 'Can I Get Out of the Bath now, Mother?'

*Year One*:  Blurred vision, bored of breasts.
*Year Two*:  Aware of older brother, not comfortable bathing with him.
*Year Three*:  Recurring dream that light switches are actually owls.
*Year Four*:  Persuade parents to move back to Ireland.
*Year Five*:  Great to be settled back in my spiritual home of Dublin. Keep on getting beaten up for being a cockney.
*Year Six*:  Brother sets fire to my pyjamas as I wear them. This

image takes over from owls. Talk parents into having another child.

*Year Seven*: Reject God.

*Year Eight*: Become altar boy.

*Year Nine*: Put poster of Che Guevara on bedroom wall.

*Year Ten*: Depressed from constant bullying. To take me away from the grim and to give me a better understanding of life, my parents take me swimming with dolphins.

The dolphins were beautiful to watch, and I became aware of their intelligence when they kept ganging up on me and dunking my head underwater.

*Year Eleven*: Start to take an interest in girls. This basically amounts to spending more time alone in my bedroom.

*Year Twelve*: Not happy having to share bath with brothers.

*Year Thirteen*: Unlucky for some. Set fire to younger brother's pyjamas . . . I was wearing them at the time.

*Year Fourteen*: Take down my Che Guevara poster on discovering that he isn't a pop star.

*Year Fifteen*: Stung by bee.

*Year Sixteen*: Leave the country for our first overseas holiday. A bit disappointed they don't stamp your passport on the Isle of Man.

*Year Seventeen*: See Robert de Niro in *Taxi Driver*. It is a revelation. His performance will never be surpassed. I have found my vocation in life.

*Year Eighteen*: Become taxi driver.

*Year Nineteen*: Mentally ill, the owls are back in my life.

*Year Twenty*: Prescribed betablockers. They don't calm me down but improve my game of snooker.

*Year Twenty-One*: Discover Milan Kundera. The expression magic realism crops up in every conversation.

*Year Twenty-Two*: Lose my virginity. Surprised the devil doesn't appear. I wouldn't say it was magical, more magic realism.

*Year Twenty-Three*: I search my house for juicy fruit only to realize I bought them in a dream. Go for a nap so I can enjoy the full flavour.

*Year Twenty-Four*: Have a near-death experience, walk past dead person.

*Year Twenty-Five*: At last, Dad tells me about the birds and the bees. I am disappointed he didn't tell me when I was stung.

*Year Twenty-Six*: Taken hostage in Iraq. I escape, freeing other hostages. I say goodbye, promising to read their autobiographies.

*Year Twenty-Seven*: I have a reunion with my two brothers. The water is a bit tepid.

*Year Twenty-Eight*: God appears before me and tells me the third secret of Fatima. Unfortunately, he raps it and I'm too shy to ask him to repeat himself.

I am asked to become the new guitarist in the pop band Suede. I decline, on the grounds that I don't want to be looking at Brett's arse all night.

Aliens land in my back garden, but I can't bring myself to forgive them ruining some freshly planted shrubs.

Play Russian roulette with Kurt Cobain. Win his sneakers. (All complaints to Courtney Love and all apologies to Kurt.)

Play former Soviet Union roulette with Boris Yeltsin. Stupidly tell him about Shannon airport duty-free prices.

Make anonymous late-night phone call to Saddam Hussein, calling him a chicken.

Send Tony Blair a copy of the Conservative manifesto.

Get drunk with O.J. Simpson, tell him he needs to get back into the limelight.

Steal shaver from Sinead O'Connor's house.

Buy 200,000 copies of 'Love is All Around Us' to give Wet, Wet, Wet a false sense of security.

Give said record to Gerry Adams. He obviously takes it to heart.

# The Grey Area

John is home in the darkness. A light bulb is powered, a spray leaving pockets of night in various corners. His shadow for company, he figures he can't stomach looking at the rented accommodation furniture. A carrier bag with frozen food and cheap wine lies beside the remote control. The night is panning out before him. A reflective realization and the notion of the beautiful girl calling at his door, looking for directions, wasn't going to happen. It is the dream that has passed many a twilight. A tiredness has him pacing the room, hovering towards the door but never reaching it as he won't break the circle. Freedom is a locked dark room, but you hold the key. He looks through his phone book as if searching for a recipe. Who to ring? The confident friend, the intellectual muse, the sweetest heart, the drugged charmer, the intense acquaintance? No, tonight he needs them all.

He notices the amount of dust on surfaces. He pops the frozen food in the oven and starts to clean his flat. He dismisses opening the wine and thinks it best to wait until the street lights come on. Duster in hand, a basin of water, a sad remembrance of his mother, little cuts on the hand, Mr Sheen seeping through his body and the thought of others keeping the catering business alive, passing passable nights and the thought of others again, alone in their clean flats, in unironed shirts, not wanting to go through the agony of sherbet speak, sucking sound-bites from durable souls and in the frenzy of cleaning, the oven noise his companion, he knows dust will gather anew. He looks to his mantelpiece, cramped with keepsakes and pinpoints the idea that he would love to hear a band, a singer honing in on a precious emotion only for a stray plastic glass to hit him on the head. Or maybe a drink with a friend with the hope of having a breakthrough in the conversation drowned in alcohol. A hyper shakiness caused by the threat of anxiety and physical manoeuvres stops the dusting. The keepsakes clean, kept for the desperate sake of reminding him that he is alive. The food is taken out of the oven, half-eaten and binned.

One phone call later, he was on the way to an old friend's house, one he hadn't see for four years, one he had lost through marriage. He reckoned it would be good to see people living under a different set of rules. He didn't believe in the compromise of marriage but it seemed to work for them. He arrived to be greeted by cats. His and her possessions had mingled into one. John was drinking a lot. The beer sat well in his half-full stomach. It was not a special occasion for the beer, it was in and out of the fridge on a daily basis. The music, the food and the couple were agreeable. The cats kept the pauses to a minimum. It was a memorable night but no photos were taken. It was time to go. They loved each other, he loved them, his love was an intrusion. He called a cab, leaving them with something to talk about.

At his front door, he has a quick look around for the lost girl. Inside, he hopes for a message on the answering machine. He calls a local friend, knowing he will be in, sitting in front of the TV with his thawed, digested food and a bottle of wine. Through telephone chat, he pulls his friend from his cheap, curvatured settee and whisks him away to the pub, not a flash pub but the shabbiest one where the mood would suit. On the way, the rain keeps heads low, there are clouds for everyone. The driver of the Datsun Sunbeam revs into a puddle, splashing a passer-by, laughter and bark crush the life from the driver. His relatives will plant another tree as a baby is born nearby. To John it was another statistic and an opening gambit in the way of small talk. Casually, flippantly, in the middle of the pub conversation, a person he deems close tears at his soul. Eyelids are batted. He pretends nothing has happened as a fireball grows within. Secretly, he makes a note not to have any contact with him again, keeping it in the part of the brain that stores all negativity, the part of the brain that can destroy a good day. He then continues the conversation, maybe he was too harsh, his eyes talk, he wants him to take it back, a hiccupped apology is called for, a Budweisered guilt, drinks all round, a mistaken mistake.

Home, a bright room to dance in, rejoice in all its purity, the light bulb goes. It is replaced by a lower wattage. Only then he notices the old one was forever flickering. He imagines the fat cat landlord cosily bouncing his children in a centrally heated family room. He curses his ineptitude in forgetting to put the wine in the fridge. He drinks it, the sickly taste contorting his face into one of his more familiar expressions. Now he feels terrible. He rings his friend again, a forgiveness is offered, half accepted and then forgotten about. A better person puts down the phone. He tries to dissect his evening. The soul likes mankind, it ventures outside, mingles, leaves the body, body loses its mind, the evening becomes regret, the soul sneaks back, blameless, the body ceases to be, the mind wants isolation, he puts on a record, the bass accompanied by the neighbours' banging, she lowers the tone. The pop song is company, shared thoughts through the safety of amplifiers, the singer sounds hurt, they bond. They don't hurt each other. They sit in rooms alone, with candles unlit, over-dramatizing their lives, hoping for quick deaths. He becomes horizontal and dismisses the world in the hope that it will dismiss him. A disturbance outside disturbs him. He lies in bed, a pain throbbing at the unlikeliest parts, a predestined pain and it hits him. He deserves to be alone as others deserve to be together and we kid ourselves because we are children.

He pushes for position, wishing the person who wasn't in bed with him would give more of the duvet, and now he will gladly open the door for anybody, hug the moment, relish the situation, put off the inevitable.

A heart attack beckons and he wants to shelter in death, to be found two weeks later, the body matching his blue eyes, the eyes that deceived many a lady and one ghastly soul. The last breath will encompass a foolish thought and it will bring a smile to his face. He dreams of his future, rushing towards the bright lights, avoiding daggers as people cheer him on. They will want to share some of the unknown with him, he becomes unknown to himself and he will get there and find it's just a bunch of lights and then the past will follow the future, resting on his mother's shoulder, gently falling asleep, her kiss will blow him to the school's gate, he will not understand the lesson, or the bullying. He will cry alone, always afraid, will rise above it, forget himself, hurt inside, express this, hurt another and cry for his mother. He feels the time is upon him, he thinks too hard, the possibility of another world is granted, hell nor heaven. He soon becomes accustomed to total darkness, is it better never to have known light? What if they throw you into this disarray, you accept it, become complacent and then they start to move the furniture around? Knowing you are there for eternity, they give you a loud clock for company. What if you escape on to a street and celebrate and you hear somebody complaining about the weather? The rain hides outside as he struggles to stay awake. Tomorrow be now, comfort him, take him away from new things, let him get to know the lost girl and then spirit him away, keep him at arm's length, let his gums and heart bleed in the brightness which is the core of his existence. His head spins and soon he becomes dead to the world.

# Bill

My brother was about to embark on a year's trip to Australia. He'd been staying with me for two months, so a tearful departure was expected. The Irish have a strange way of saying goodbye. The night before it's a beery 'I love you, I'll really miss you' session. The morning brings the frailest of hugs followed by a swift 'See ya', and absolutely under no circumstance is there to be any eye contact. The accepted form of showing emotion is not to show any emotion. It is understood that the tears have to fall in solitude. I felt a tremendous sadness and within minutes I was on the phone to the Battersea Dogs Home. They said they were really sorry to hear about my brother but explained that they kept dogs. I decided to get one. The thought of shouting 'Here boy' and a lovely creature running into my arms caused such an impulse.

This wasn't a rash decision. I'd been planning to get a dog for eight years. The urge comes and goes, usually late at night after playing with somebody else's dog. I feel it's the same urge some women get when around others' children. At least I don't have to go through the hassle of meeting someone, falling in love, procreating and waiting for nine months. The procedure for getting a dog is visiting the Home, filling out a questionnaire, being house assessed and then going back to pick a dog. Here now beside me sits my dog Bill. I have had him three days and he is in need of constant attention. He wants to play – 'play' in his dictionary meaning: attempt to take owner's arm out of socket. He keeps trying to sit on me, and I put him down, explaining I have to finish this article. 'Somebody has to bring home the Chum.'

The questionnaire had some bizarre questions, the strangest one being – 'Why do you want a dog?' How can you possibly answer that? To kill the cat next door . . . because I've got no friends . . . I eventually put 'To shower with affection'. Having done this, the House Assessor calls to my home. As expected, he has a beard. This is a bit like going through customs: you try to act as normal as possible but come across as a dog killer.

After some canine bonding we got on the subject of traffic congestion in London. He did most of the talking as I don't drive. Out of the blue he said I was suitable. I think it was my reference to roadworks on the North Circular that swung it. Before he left he insisted on giving me some helpful tips like 'When choosing a dog, if he comes over and licks you that's a good sign.' I decide to go first thing on Monday morning. He tells me that's not such a good idea as families tend to go at the weekend, leaving the dregs for the beginning of the week. That suits me fine as I like the idea of having a dog that nobody else wants.

On arriving at Battersea I became nervous at the responsibility of it all. Also the socialist in me questions the ethics of the situation: giving a roof and food to a dog when the homeless problem is reaching epidemic proportions. When a dog does a trick we give him a biscuit – surely a tramp could come in and sing us a song, for the same reward? Then I figured you can never get a tramp to lick your face.

The first dog we saw had my friend in tears. Outside each cage there is a card with details of the creature. Whoever writes these will never get a job in public relations. They state things like 'A bit freaky, very randy, not suitable for first time owners'. I think of the fun of defacing these, of an old couple falling in love with a poodle, only to read: 'Quite a friendly dog, very toy oriented, has a habit of attacking old people'. The dogs know the score and make a huge effort to grab your attention – you expect to turn a corner to see one of them juggling. (I was about to pick him, but then he dropped one.) Others have that 'I don't want to live with you' look. After an hour I took a card down to the office saying which one I wanted, only to be told it wasn't suitable for me. The only thing I knew for certain was that I didn't want a Jack Russell. Our family pet Patch was one. She was the kind of dog that would sit on your lap for an hour and if you dared to stroke her she'd have your arm off.

After another hour of reading cards and looking at sad eyes, I'm down to the final three. I ask to see them in their swimsuits. Obviously as far as Bill is concerned he was always first choice (unlike adopted kids I think it's best he doesn't know). Having made my choice, the reality of the moment hadn't set in. I feel I must be like those men who continually go out with similar looking women, because I picked a Jack Russell, well a cross between a Jack Russell and a Lord knows what. Lord knows whats are renowned for shagging anything that moves. As the handler goes to get the dog, the same question keeps probing my mind. Why do you want a dog? It seems to me it's because it would be my dog. If I was to be honest with myself, I would have to say I was Patch's fourth favourite family member. This was my opportunity to be a dog's favourite person in the world. It's a pity there wasn't enough space on that questionnaire. The dog comes to me, I beckon for him to jump on my lap. He lands on top of my head. Is this a good sign? After taking him for a walk I now know Bill is a cross between a Jack Russell and a greyhound. I'm soon to be the laughing stock of the neighbourhood. 'There goes that fast dog, who's that fella dragging along the ground after him?' I'm told it's important to build up his confidence as he has been in the Home for over eight months. I try my best by saying things like 'Are those your real eyelashes? You've got lovely paws. Hey, nice ass!'

We're still at the stage where we're sussing each other out. It's all new to both of us. I've certainly never been woken up at seven in the morning with a canine sitting on my face before. And as for my foolish idea that he would be grand protector of our castle, after three days I still haven't heard him bark and that's despite me shouting 'KILL!' every time the doorbell goes. The only way he's going to stop a burglar is by sniffing him to death. He's also learnt that trick of pretending there's an intruder in the garden last thing at night.

People love dogs because they're so similar to us. You hear stories about dogs who start to look like their owners. Where we are frightened of turning into our parents, I think Bill, after three days with me, like most dogs, is frightened of turning into his owner. The thing I'm really still looking forward to is me saying 'Here boy' and him running into my arms. This should happen once he eventually leaves my side.

# We Can Beat Them Just for One Day

Music has always provided us with our fair share of heroes, those people who have sacrificed commercial reward for artistic integrity and at the same time guided us through the tricky parts of our lives. Music ties us together (couples have their song) and tears us apart (the Iggy Pop album is mine, I'm taking it with me). Certain songs act as memory aids to our past. I was listening to 'Nightporter' by Japan when I had my first anxiety attack. We all relate certain events to particular tunes. Of late I've been listening to The Frank and Walters, A House and The Divine Comedy, names you won't be familiar with but all special in their own way. Their music has lilted itself into my life and been given a place in my heart and on my stereo. The point being, I come not to praise these sung heroes but to bury them in this piece.

With so many bands vying for our attention, who is it that decides which ones are worthy of a record deal? These three bands came into the world via a bicycle courier, namely Keith Cullen. I want to applaud this man for taking off the bicycle clips and donning the guise of the record company, Setanta. We often hear tales of visionaries who start their own company and after years of hard slog now front multi-national conglomerates. Keith started small in April 1989 and now after years of back-breaking labour remains small. The label's first release, from a band called Beethoven, went on to sell 200 copies. The big record companies might well laugh, but that's 200 people whose musical tastes were not being catered for by them. Keith lost money on this first venture and is still in debt to this day. You must wonder what keeps the man going.

He runs the office from his small flat in South London with his two chums, Fergal and Simon. He has the fax machine on top of the fridge, the Macintosh on the oven, and the AGM is held in the bathroom, the only bonus of the crammed space being that it cuts down on travel expenses. Besides the day-to-day office duties, he has to listen to endless demo tapes in the hope that one might be worth checking out. The problem being the biggies are always sniffing around too, which is where Keith's cycling skills come in handy.

Most new bands start with a handful of raw songs and the arrogance of youth coupled with the expectation that they will be the next big thing. They want to go to the biggest company possible. This seems to make sense. You are given a pile of money – this is called an advance and they expect it back pretty sharpish. They will then put a big marketing team behind you, give you a more saleable image and will allow you to work with a well-known, over-priced record producer.

If you ask politely, they may well put you on a nice health plan and pension scheme. There is also the added incentive that you might get to share the same label as Michael Bolton. What can Keith offer you in comparison? Firstly, it is harder to get on Setanta than it is Sony because the simple point is that Keith will only sign bands that he personally likes. Once you're in, the man sweats blood for you and, more importantly, he puts his money where his mouth is. This is all done on a verbal agreement, meaning that any of the bands can leave at any given time. This doesn't happen because loyalty plays a big part within the organization. About his band The Divine Comedy, Keith said he would be willing to rob houses to ensure that the records got released. Having heard the record myself, I might well give him a hand or at least keep look-out. The record in question is 'Liberation' and was easily my favourite release of 1993. I salute Keith for bringing to my attention such a gem. In an industry fuelled by ego and money it is refreshing to know someone who sees his job as nurturing these bands, giving them enough space to make mistakes even though he faces bankruptcy on a daily basis. It is heartening that a young underdog can still place little things of beauty on to the market place sandwiched between the corp-rock banalities dished out by the majors. This is what independent music is all about, not the four spaced-out, loud-shirted guitar-heads who bide their time on the conveyor belt waiting for the big deal. Let the corporations go over the minutes from their last meeting and worry about ganging up to maintain the over-pricing of CDs, or cause devastation with their whimsical dropping of bands unable to meet the accountant's musical taste. It is important that there are people in the industry like Keith who care about the music as much as the musicians themselves.

# Entitled

The lost look is the one I seek
not to be found at the usual outlets
you have brushed past me in dreams
remaining untouched
making a mockery of my world
the thought of our laid-back
cynical depressed togetherness
makes me want to jump for joy
please come soon

I will find you as the sky is about to break
that moment when the sun and the rain
do battle
when the clouds can't settle on a colour
where shadows terrorize us
insanity rates soar
and humans become aware of their
insignificance
we look upwards for answers
realizing things aren't black and white
I will find you then
we will live in this grey area
not happy but aware
and we will feel no need to chat about the
weather.

# A Weekend at Champneys

It's Friday night, a night when traditionally people shake off their shackles, pig out, drink themselves into dizzying heights and boogie away their problems. It's time to liberate the week through excess. I find myself in bed before midnight, nicely tucked up with a chest cold dreaming of my visit to the health farm tomorrow morning. It couldn't come at a better time as I have let myself go a little over the last twenty-eight years. I figured my weekend away should just about do the trick. At five in the morning I'm simply dreaming of dreaming.

Three hours' sleep later and we're on our way. A friend has agreed to come on this spying mission with me. We arrive at eleven with strong resolve and good intention and park our clapped-out car in between a Jaguar and a Rolls-Royce. The grounds are rather splendid and the interior looks much like a grand hotel. The one difference being all the guests look like inmates from *One Flew Over the Cuckoo's Nest*, they walk around in a robotic fashion wearing long white robes, and when the receptionist said we should go and see Sister, I checked to see that the front door hadn't been locked behind us. The duty manager John, an unhealthy affable type, took us on a tour of the resort. First stop was the smoking room and then on to all the facilities: gym, pool, sauna, art-made-easy class, tummy trimming room, games area, restaurant and gift shop. To give John his due, he tried to make it interesting – without much success. 'This is the pool, this is where people swim, there's some towels over there. This is the sauna, this is where people get very hot, there's some towels over there.' John was very proud of the amount of towels they use (officially 1,750 a day).

A quick fag and it was time to meet Sister. Any sort of check-up frightens me. I always expect them, after consulting their charts, to say, 'It's not looking good, Mr Hughes. In fact, according to my notes, you're dead!' I was slightly disappointed to find my blood pressure was normal. One decaff coffee later and we decide to ease ourselves into this health lark with a game of ping pong followed by pool. I'm feeling better already.

Lunch time and the restaurant is divided into two sections – normal and dieting. The staff are very helpful. 'Excuse me, fat person, you're in the wrong section.' The tiniest of partitions separates them. I was a bit put out that there wasn't a looks-like-death-warmed-up category. They operate a buffet service which shows you the number of calories per item. It kind of takes the fun out of eating but, regardless, I had some 400 calories, with a side order of 150 calories, and a 250 calories dessert.

I was booked in for heat treatment next. I approached the desk with intrepidation. A little old man said I could have sauna or steam. I opted for steam. 'Just take off your robe and shut the door behind you.' I lasted forty seconds. Thankfully I was alone, because on religious grounds I'm not allowed to sit beside other naked men in case I get homoerotic fantasies thereafter. Next up was my massage. The young lady told me to keep my boxers on. I tried to make small talk so as not to get aroused. Luckily she was very clinical in her approach. All the same, when she started slapping my legs in that kung fu motion, the noise made me want to shout out 'WAYHAY!' Only another five hours before dinner, so we have a slim-fit banana bar which seems to disintegrate before it reaches my mouth.

I forgot to bring togs with me, but the gift shop sells them for a very unreasonable £30. They are a hundred per cent polyamide. Over a cigarette my friend warns me that if I could see my lungs I'd quit smoking. I point out that if I could see my lungs I'd have approximately three seconds to live, just enough time to light up. I've never been to a gym before, but on entering this one it was how I expected. I tried the bicycle machine, the steps, rowing and the one with weights you push with your arms that makes you all shaky after two goes. Gillie, the General Manager, on seeing me struggle over one weight, enthused about the amount I could lift if I was here a full week. I somehow don't think it's a skill that I'll need. 'Excuse me, Mr Removal Man, let me lift that heavy box for you. I've been to Champneys, I'm qualified.'

Gillie used to be an air hostess and it showed. She was a female Desmond Lynam. They must have gone to the same Speak Calm, Look Concerned soothing school. 'Try to relaaax' was her catch phrase. She's the person you want beside you on your dying bed. 'Sean, we're just going to turn off your life support machine, try to relaaax.' After an hour's work-out, it's time for the footy results, a nap and *Brookside*. Only two hours to dinner. I watch *Noel's House Party* and maybe it's the pangs of hunger that are making me hallucinate but I really think Noel enjoys doing the show, he actually likes running around punning to his heart's content, playing little japes on the all-consuming public. He probably had a terrible childhood – God love him.

My chest cold has moved up to my head, so I sneeze away the next hour. My friend forgoes saying 'Bless you' after about twenty minutes. We're first down for dinner and I manage to barter an extra roll for an autograph. Their butter portions cover a quarter of the roll at a stretch. 700 calories heavier and I'm back in the smoking room. A woman who has been coming for twenty years sits comfortably smoking an expensive cigar. She offers information about her wealth unabashed. 'I don't use the sauna or pool because we have them at home.' They obviously don't have chairs then. Two young ladies from Harrow tell of their secret stash of mince pies they smuggled in. The conversation gets on to chocolate and one person reminisces about 1977 when apparently there was a chocolate mousse on the menu, it was very light though. We had a midnight swim at 10 p.m., the whole pool to ourselves. It was glorious, I contemplate selling my soul, doing a TV advert and owning my own pool. I decide against it. I go to bed hungrily wondering if polyamide is edible.

A good night's sleep and I check to see what Champney's thought for the day is. This is their little message which they plaster all over the premises. It reads 'The mind is like a flower, it is beautiful when it is open.' I came with an open mind, but I feel this place is more suited to people trying to lose weight in a pampered but painful fashion regardless of price.

The facilities are excellent and the greatest joy was using the outdoor jacuzzi in sub-zero temperatures. Your body delights in the warm bubbles as your face turns blue. Champneys is S&M for the rich without the hassle of bondage. It did open my eyes to my excesses, but it seems the more concerned you are about your health the less fun your life will become. Jumping on the weighing scales after a week here, the only thing you're likely to lose is your sense of humour. So it's back to my moderate civilization, and remember: 'The pub is like a flower, it is beautiful when it is open.'

# How's Your Show Going?

I've decided to write this piece in the style of the Edinburgh festival itself. The initial excitement, the buzz, quick look at the programme, look who's on: Malcolm Hardy; revues with silly names; *The Wow Show* is back; your chance to see four different versions of *Abigail's Party*; and not forgetting the opportunity to catch some of your favourite TV advertisement personalities doing stand-up comedy. What else has Edinburgh got to offer? The Brazilian rain forest of leaflets thrust into your hand, the jugglers on the street looking for new variations on throwing objects into the air (and yet they object when I throw stuff at them), the tourists walking into a Fringe show by mistake and being too embarrassed to leave, the entire population of Edinburgh becoming critics for the duration, the Mr Benn transformation of certain venues – usually a poky wine cellar but for the festival an exclusive atmospheric theatre. The lies of Tardis proportions when it comes to flats: 'an extremely large, well-furnished, three-bedroomed house' is, in fact, a poky wine cellar.

What does the festival offer the newcomer? Many will have seen television programmes professing to show the highlights of the Fringe. Don't believe them. They offer a bastardized version of events: 'I know your show is a conceptual monologue, but could we lift three minutes of it, please?' First time performers shouldn't be fooled by the scores of television employees running around like headless television employees looking for the next big thing – they just clutter up the audience, desperately trying to gauge reactions without understanding any of your jokes. As for awards, there seem to be about twenty on offer, and new ones appear every year. 'Henley's Bakery is proud to announce its Best Thing Since Sliced Bread Award. This is a prestigious award for performers who are doing Edinburgh in the vain hope of getting their own TV series rather than because they feel they have something to say.' The more awards, the better; it's a step in the right direction. Lose the competitive nature, give everyone a prize. Having said that, I feel I have a fair chance of winning the Sean Hughes award this year. Apparently, it's between myself and Karl McDermott.

Week two starts and a sense of *déjà vu* sets in, but I'm sure you've heard that before. Am I bumping into the same people in the same place every night? And are we having the same conversation? I now know where they got the idea for the film *Groundhog Day*.

From a performing point of view, three weeks is a bit of a strain; it's all right if the show's going well but, if it's a disaster, the festival can seem as long as a . . . very long thing (sorry, I gave up after an hour of trying to think of funny long things). In week two most of the reviews filter through: this is the time when you have to avoid friends who have been given bad ones. You just have to wave at them from a distance, pointing at your watch as if in a hurry. If you find they, too, are making similar gestures, the paranoia sets in, so you buy all the papers and magazines and lock yourself in a room. The other sign of a bad review is if you see somebody with a fixed grin and an 'I'm not hurt' look on their face. Comics tend to dismiss bad reviews but secretly re-read them all the time, even looking up certain words to make sure nothing is misunderstood.

Reviews aren't that important in Edinburgh – word of mouth is what sells tickets. One year I did a show with Steve Frost: 'A scathing attack on the world of media', we realized it was about, after the critics had their say. We thought it was just a knockabout comedy. You live and learn. On another occasion, a play I was doing with Owen O'Neill, *Patrick's Day*, got such an horrendous review we blew it up and stuck it on to the door so that punters could see it as they came in. We even used some of the lines as part of the play.

By the last week, you care less about how your show is going and more about making sure you're not the last one out of the Gilded Balloon bar. The only way you can guarantee this is if Arthur Smith is also present. I haven't missed Edinburgh for the last five years. This time I'm only doing four nights, making sure word of mouth doesn't kill it off. I love the spirit of the festival, it's unique in every sense. To me, it's about the mix of hundreds of shows all baying for your attention, and this is why I'm worried by the coming together of three of the larger venues – the Gilded Balloon, the Assembly Rooms and the Pleasance – as a single entity. These three have always done good things, but I feel that, if the punters think they can see everything at these places, the smaller ones will go to the wall. The nightmare scenario is that the bigger venues and promoters will gain a monopoly – a few people will be making all the decisions, the prices may go up and the content will be less diverse. I don't mind though as long as I get to be the little car.

Certainly go to these venues but, remember, the most fun is checking out those poky wine cellars.

SEAN'S 10 THINGS TO WATCH OUT FOR AT THE FESTIVAL

* Malcolm Hardy's Bollocks
* Comics buying drinks for the Montreal Festival representatives
* The *Guardian* going all gooey-eyed over anything remotely American
* Seeing if Avalon can make their posters any bigger
* The *Glasgow Herald* giving the most informative reviews
* Karen Koren shouting at her staff at the Gilded Balloon
* Mark Steele being overlooked by the Perrier panel again
* Quality papers coming over as passionate about comedy at the festival but ignoring it for the rest of the year
* The realization that the door staff at every venue are illegal Australians
* Watching the Montreal Festival representatives falling over drunk

# The Black 'n' White Page

Confused people should stop at this juncture
and write your own shit

I Kiss you via the third person
It's the only way I know
their salt and taste
and cheap perfume
getting in the way
and all you say is
at least they bloody shaved

A loved one writes to a prisoner
He tells her that she's a ███████
and he will always ███████ her
She is pleased that the prison warden
is thinking of her

the gold digger sees the glistening shiny object
his machine makes excited noises
his heart rate soars
his penis tingles
his underpants are too tight
another milk bottle top for his collection
slightly to his left buried deep in the soil
is a treasure which will remain buried

a compromise is the state content people
don't know they're in.

Black and White mixed makes a sort of grey.
The painter was happy with his colour scheme
as he gulped from the bottle of Kaliber.

# Super Sub

I've always had a tremendous love for the game of football. My Dad took me to my first game when I was four. The result was Arsenal 5, Wolves 1, a classic by all accounts. This game impressed me so much my next one came eighteen years later. I think this is my only failing as an ambassador for the sport: I find it dull to watch. I love the idea of football, teams winning and losing, going up and down the league, the transfers, the sending-offs, the robotic post-match interviews, the chanting of the crowd, the 'if only' pub conversations, the radio commentators' over-the-top rantings. But more than anything I love that quarter-to-five feeling on a Saturday as the results come in. As a child I was offered the chance to see Arsenal play or be given 10 pence. I have now saved £75.60 which is about how much it costs to sit in Highbury these days. I never went to the games but I never missed falling asleep in front of *Match of the Day* every Saturday night. I also bought the magazine *Shoot* every Wednesday. I would cut out pictures of players and make up elaborate games in my head. I can honestly say at age eight I invented fantasy football. When we moved to Ireland my obsession grew, knowing that I couldn't see live football anymore.

Around this time I busied myself actually playing football. I was in the local team, I had the mighty number 12 emblazoned on my back. I don't know if it was my paranoia, but I'm sure the manufacturers make that number slightly bigger than the others. I rarely got a game and, if so, I was usually put in goal. You could say I didn't see eye to eye with the manager. He was my Dad. I retired from the game at age twelve, hoping to get into coaching (no, that's just football speak). My decision came after a particular game which saw me as an outfield player. I was in defence, and my understanding of the game was tackle and boot it up the other end as soon as possible. If it happened to land at the feet of one of our players I laid claim to precision passing but, realistically, passing wasn't part of my game plan. During this gruelling match there was an almighty goalmouth scramble at their end.

I happened to be up there for some reason, I think I forgot to change over at half-time, but rather than hitting a simple tap in, the ball kind of bounced off my foot (well, my thigh to be exact), and into the goal. I had scored. At this point the rest of the team put me on their shoulders and chaired me up and down the pitch. I know their hearts were in the right place but unfortunately *to patronize* was already firmly in my vocabulary.

I was never any good at sport; I was small, skinny, unhealthy and unsociable, perfect for cross-country running. I did have a brief flirtation with boxing, not through choice I might add. One of the kids over the road had been given boxing gloves by his parents. This was a dilemma as these were the only pair of gloves in the neighbourhood but, as luck would have it, I was the only left-handed person within a ten-mile radius. Our bouts went something like this: he'd call for me, we'd put on one glove each, he'd punch me very hard in the face, I'd go in crying and we'd arrange the time of the next day's bout.

I duly went back to my football fixation. I tried my darndest to take an interest in League of Ireland football, but the idea of spending wet Sundays watching twenty-two fat blokes, in varying degrees of fitness, slip and slide their way through ninety minutes, just didn't grab me. I did catch the results and follow the tables, but not with much enthusiasm. To me Sunday afternoons were about sitting on the couch with my family watching *The Big Match*. I do have the utmost respect for the few thousand fanatics who go to League of Ireland games, these are the people who will tell you that there is nothing like the atmosphere of a live game. But I find, with the minimum of effort, football can be just as exciting in your own home. What I do to create this atmosphere is to sit on a very uncomfortable chair and stick a big pole in front of the television, then I get my neighbour to sit in front of me with his chair firmly pressed into my knees while wearing a big bobble hat. Personally I think I'd more willingly listen to Brian Moore's commentary rather than take the risk of sitting beside someone who shouts 'Cunt!' a lot. But that's parents for you.

Each week we were spoilt for choice: Liverpool, Leeds, Manchester United, Tottenham. I could support any of these. I plumped for Crystal Palace, a lowly third division side at the time. While the other kids would rant on about cup finals, my Monday morning conversation was, 'One-all away to Mansfield, can't complain.' I bought programmes, flags, pendants, I scoured the sports pages for information, but isn't that what football's all about – that sense of belonging? I go to see Palace play regularly now, it's an hour and a half drive. I don't go with the anticipation of seeing some brilliant football, it's more from a sense of warped loyalty.

Football at its most important is not about winning or losing, it's more about nil-all draws. It's about bringing a community together, and people from all different walks of life cheering their team on. They may be crap but they're our crap. The last World Cup saw Ireland competing and even if they had lost every game they were always sure of an open-top bus reception waiting for them at Dublin airport. I watched the games in London, and it was fun to hear the pundits pontificate on how if England had qualified they would have walked it. It was also fun to see how they reacted to the Irish games. For the first game they were simply the Republic of Ireland; after a win they became the team from the British Isles. I hate to think what would have happened had we actually won the World Cup, I'm sure the British media would have claimed the whole country back. My big hope for the future of football is that it will remain as the focal point of the community, that Crystal Palace will qualify for Europe and that one day a British commentator will manage to pronounce Paul McGrath's name properly.

# Booze Daze

It has been drawn to my attention that I may have been drinking a tad too much of late. Never to the extent of having a problem but enough to start asking questions. Yes, the mind is willing to have another, luckily the body knows its limitations. As an exercise in discipline, I find myself in my local public house at 8 p.m., ordering an orange juice. I feel like an athlete before the big race: 'Come on Sean, pull yourself together, it's all about discipline, you can do it. Here's some steroids.' I decided to do this alone as there is no fate worse than watching your friends get steadily more drunk. It's not the idea of them having a better time than you, it's that realization that your friends are assholes – the sadder implication being that you're an asshole yourself because you have never noticed before.

How to pass the time? I get change for the slot machine, juke box, pool table and condom dispenser. This being more or less an old man's pub, the only justification I can think of for the condom machine is to remind the punters that sex still exists. All goes well as I busy myself reading a book at the same time as trying not to look like I've been stood up, a skill I've acquired over the years as have many others in this particular pub. We nod sheepishly at each other, which around these parts is commonly known as a sad man's handshake.

On reflection, I was never one for those beery nights where come the next morning the guys boast of the eighteen pints they downed. We have eight pints of water in our body as it is. Surely after eighteen more you would start to resemble the Michelin man. Even in my wild excesses, four pints was the crossover point before I went on to shorts. As a teen, I was keen to try out every short until I found the one to suit me – meaning the one I didn't throw up on. Bailey's is the only option I have left. To be fair, Pernod had a good innings. My parents' carpet is a legacy of my youthful exuberance.

I find I can't concentrate on the book, but, well prepared for this eventuality, have brought a paper with me. I already feel healthier and must admit that the tell-tale signs of my hobby were becoming apparent. Ones like having a heart to heart with a friend while he thinks you are doing an impression of Bob Dylan, and panic attacks when the last bell is called. The final straw came when my local publicans invited me round for Christmas Dinner. I have now read the newspaper cover to cover. I decide to read it again, this time taking in the foreign news properly and having a quick glimpse at the property page. I toy with the idea of having a beer.

I know I could never become one of those 24-hour drinkers. I have tasted 'Tennent's Super' and what a wonderful sense of irony the makers have. To bring the Catholic Church into the twentieth century, I feel this delicacy should replace wine at every church ceremony. That would really test the priest's faith. I have resolve, however, and decide to stay with the orange juice.

I have now done both crosswords, tried to understand the chess puzzle, read the beer mat half a dozen times and started to play that game where you put half the beer mat over the edge of the table and flick it up in the air in the hope of catching it. I then order every flavour of crisps available. 'Willpower, Sean, you're doing great, think positive.' The thought nags at me that I haven't really enjoyed getting drunk in a long time. It goes from those first few rushed drinks to falling over bins and apologizing to them. I ask for the darts and chat for too long to the woman collecting for cancer research. It's soon time for peanuts. I rejoice in the idea of not having a hangover or those character-building moments of boozy regret, waking up in the morning with no recollection of the night before but with the name Louise firmly planted in my mind. 'Louise, Louise, what happened with Louise?' It was only then that I saw lying beside me some big, fat, hairy biker with Louise tattooed on his arse.

Much to the barmaid's distaste, I have now torn up at least twelve beer mats and have started to people-watch, my head turning automatically each time the door opens. I am feeling good as memories of my Dad coming home from the pub justify my sobriety. The rest of the family would be enjoying a cosy suburban night in front of the television. In he would stumble with five minutes of the film left. Hate would fill the room, he'd switch to another channel and quickly fall asleep. I suppose this was our Tennent's Super moment. We would fume, wish we were adults, lock away grudge points and promise not to treat our future kids that way. It was worse if he was in a good mood, because then we would be allowed to watch the movie but with his continual interruptions. 'Who's he? Why did he do that? Who's she? Who's he? Is he dead? What did she just say?' at which point the movie would be over.

Back at the pub, I've started to crumple crisp packets into tight squares so they fit snugly into the ashtray. As they unfold, I burn holes in them with my cigarette, mentally clocking 'that's the next thing I'm giving up'. I've never really liked crisps anyway. I watch the last of the remaining ice dissolve in my glass and contemplate buying the remaining three packets of peanuts to see the young model's undergarments. No alcohol and I'm still having fun.

The pub quiz has just started. I don't join in, but as they give the answers at the end of each round, I continually shout 'Yes!', mocking their competitiveness while they admire my supposed knowledge of trivia. Feeling a tremendous sense of achievement, I decide to call it a night. I look down smugly on all these weak souls who need alcohol. I catch a glimpse of the pub's clock. It's five past eight. 'Do you do Supers on draught please?'

# Men Trapped in Men's Bodies

Dear The Smiths,

It's nigh on impossible to say anything about them which hasn't been said before. I could say they come from Portugal, but there's been enough lies written about them already. Seven albums and four living legends later and the myths roll on. It's hard to understand why this collection has been re-packaged, it's harder still to comprehend why there are people out there who haven't got these records. Well this is for you, you've read the blurb, now listen to the music. What will you get? Probably more than you bargained for: a rich vein of humour, heartfelt lyrics, a sense of belonging and some cracking tunes. It's like finding an old love letter. The records say it all, we don't need any Johnny Rogan type books or gossip mongers, let's just leave them be and instead thank them for gracing us with their genius.

When they first came on the scene I was eighteen years old going on six. I remember them creating quite a stir at the time, but I have this terrible habit of missing the boat when it comes to music. I bought my first Talking Heads album about a year ago. Somebody told me about 'This Charming Man' and I was warned that they were a bit depressing to listen to. Of course, being a moron, I took this on board myself and when-ever anyone mentioned them, without ever having heard a note, I'd say in my irritating teenage whine, 'The Smiths, they're crap, they just drone on and on.' I think secretly I was in love with them even then. It was a strange one really, as they were the perfect band for me. I wasn't exactly an out-going teenager: when everyone else spent their Saturday nights playing at being couples, I stayed in my bedroom eating chocolate fingers feeling sorry for myself. I needed company, and somehow putting Spandau Ballet's 'True' on the turntable didn't seem to do the trick. Unfortunately, *Top of the Pops* was the juke box for this suburban Dublin kid's life, and all the while The Smiths were articulating feelings too close for comfort. I curse my ignorance.

'Hatful of Hollow' came out and my friend bought it because it was a mid-price album – he was a bit of a miser and only bought cheap records. We used to sit in his bedroom and play it over and over, and I had this sneaky respect for it. In fact, 'Please, Please, Please Let Me Get What I Want' used to send shivers up my spine. This could also have something to do with the fact that my friend's parents never turned on the heating in his room during the day.

Around this time, I was in a crap double act and I once sang 'I would go out tonight but I've got this big tree up my arse' while dancing around the stage with a big tree up my arse. 'Meat is Murder' I missed completely as I had just dropped out of society and we were rarely up for *Top of the Pops* and then too doped out of it to find the radio. My little fling with The Smiths was over as we at the commune listened to somebody's Billy Bragg record continually. It was the only music we had. We would all gather round and reminisce about the first time we heard Billy Bragg; of course, this was my first time hearing it. I bought my first Billy Bragg record about two years ago. Here we were living on the 15th floor of a damp high-rise building, surrounded by heroin addicts in rainy Elephant and Castle, living on beans and I had the cheek to ask 'Has anyone heard the "Meat is Murder" LP?' 'The Smiths! They're too depressing,' they chorused. Morrissey would have laughed, us being vegetarians without even knowing.

'The Queen is Dead' found me in Ireland again, and I still didn't have any of their records and had never seen them live, but I was still a sort of a fan. I was making a living playing a wacky barman on a television pop show at the time. It was mind-numbingly dull. The guests included Maxi Priest and Erasure, but then The Smiths arrived and I was to share a dressing-room with them. Seeing them perform live – well, miming – was mesmerizing. The fans went wild and I was getting goose bumps down my neck and they were only playing 'Shoplifters of the World Unite'. I was now a fan. I wanted to say hello, but I can't talk to people just for the sake of it.

I knew Morrissey liked Oscar Wilde, so I spent all night trying to think up a clever question to ask him. After about two hours I was confident enough with my query and popped into the dressing-room to find they were gone. No note or anything.

I was back in London for the 'World Won't Listen' album, which was quite apt as I'd just started doing comedy in the clubs and was regularly getting heckled off the stage. Being penniless, I made use of the existing library services to borrow this record all the time. This wasn't much of a problem as The Eurythmics seemed to be the most popular band in the Turnpike Lane area. You would be surprised how many comics love The Smiths. I don't know how many times I've dined out on my 'I shared a dressing-room with them' story. Well, it was more take-aways really.

'Strangeways Here We Come', which is my personal favourite, was the time I caught up with them – I actually bought the record on release. I publicly showed my love, I was a statistic in their record sales. The excitement of it all caused them to split up. I wonder would the same thing happen if I bought a Pearl Jam record? It's worth a try.

I sometimes think it's wrong to buy your favourite records, and I still haven't gotten around to getting all of The Smiths' stuff. If you can put them on at a whim, the novelty wears off. Imagine the joy of driving in a car and 'Girlfriend in a Coma' comes on the radio. Out of the blue you remember what a great song it is.

I've never seen them live, but 'Rank' is a pretty good substitute. In a sense, I'm glad I didn't see them as the actual event never lives up to the expectation. Much like this collection has to live up to the hype. It does, but in an understated way. The Smiths grow on you, offering little snippets of life, dealing with real emotions, with the music fusing in, to make the words and the instrumentation inseparable. I don't think we'll see its like again. Morrissey won't make you happy, he'll make you aware. They have certainly made my life richer. Recently I met up with Morrissey and he quoted a line from *Sean's Show* where I say 'Everybody gets over their Morrissey phase – well, except Morrissey that is.' 'Too true,' he added. Of course he is wrong, for as we know, he will continually write words that say something about our lives. Goodbye The Smiths and Hello Morrissey, Marr, Joyce and Rourke.

A fan.

PS. Better late than never. Buy some of these records, you 'miss the boat' types. Now who's that band Nirvana that everyone's talking about?

# A Night in Phoning Ex-Lovers

Although you pleaded for your space
you are given your own space
the night starts planless
you are free
you fall into doing what you normally do
this time alone ·

you enjoy your own company
(methinks before getting down to it)
and you arrange to meet the past
not contemplating it will be the future
when it's the now you are trying to satisfy
and you know she is the everything
but you have been given a life that lies to you
so you want everything and a bit more

and it is only because time passes
that you oblige temptation
aware that if the shoe was on the other foot
it would hurt
and random thoughts are flying
goodbye and crush me
and fingertip length hugs aren't called for
but that touch is needed on occasion, now
Why? maybe it's my two-week holiday

and yes you could write this
and only the ones who can
can take pleasure

and don't park that car on a double yellow line
I don't love you but I wish you no malice or fines
left with the anticipation that the phone will ring
to disturb you
running a second ahead of time

## A Night in Phoning Ex-Lovers

and when I love me I am capable
of loving you

I will wear jumpers for you
without rhyme nor reason
and isn't that our lives

poems should be written in isolation
only next door wants to drill
because the drill wants its say as well
and like the leaves fallen only noticed
when fell

I give this lazily to you
but Jesus haven't I overheard
all my philosophies
and outsiders can't spoil this
and now I need to ring my mother
but she's engaged.

# Night with Grown-ups

I've hit that age now when I'm too old to be young and too young to be old. It's the age when you start getting invited to dinner parties. Not many, though, as a single person tends to stick out on these occasions. I usually end up going to about two a year, purely as a social exercise, to see what couples talk about in company. As people start introducing me to their partners, I introduce them to my bottle of wine: 'Hi, I'm Sean and this is Domaine St Pierre Chardonnay 1993'.

I was told proceedings would start at 8 o'clock. I figured at dinner parties they'd be a punctual lot and I didn't want to be late, or to lose my 'I've got things to do' persona. So, weighing it all up with the help of graphs and calculators, I decided to arrive at 8.32, having had my coat on and been ready to go since half past four. I knock on the door. 'Sorry I'm . . . first here?'

Their kid is still up. I am introduced to her and quickly forget her name. I get on very well with children. They seem to want to play with me, sensing that I'm not really a grown-up. A few more guests arrive. Out of shyness, I play more intensely with their little girl. I ask my host if I can smoke. She says we had better wait until the kid goes to bed. I stop playing with her immediately. More people arrive, and as they come in I find everyone is standing up and it's like that feeling in church when you think you might have missed a bit, so I just stand with them, feel awkward and sit down again. I'm introduced to everybody and we mutually pay no attention to each other's names. I think it's so that I can have the embarrassment later on of saying, 'Hey, you in the specs, pass the salt please.'

As everyone gets settled, the topicality section of the evening begins and everyone starts talking about the IRA ceasefire. This is where the Irish accent comes in handy, because no matter what drivel you speak, you will be granted a certain amount of authority. I waffle on about Republican splinter groups, the difference between Sinn Fein and the IRA, the obvious assurance that Sinn Fein has got from America, the possibilities of civil war, the calling in of the UN . . . I even start to believe myself. Then I do my big joke about the voice-over actors going out of business and how Martin McGuinness is impossible to dub. I don't realize we have stopped talking about the ceasefire and we are on to the magician David Copperfield. I say, 'Magic's all very well, but did you know that Gerry Adams has actually served time in prison?' It being a media party, they don't tell me to shut up, but for the rest of the night I am played by an actor.

The last of the guests telephones asking for directions, as he is stuck on a motorway miles away, only to ring on the door a moment later. The portable phone has taken the practical joke a step further. Soon, everybody finishes their glass of champagne. Now, don't get the wrong impression, I despise what champagne stands for, its crass association with success. To me, alcohol is there purely to serve its purpose as a substance to numb the mind, not as a status symbol. By law, champagne should only be served to winning Grand Prix racing drivers. Onwards to dinner, or, as I call it, a distraction before the real drinking starts. Food isn't high on my agenda and, seeing that I'm vegetarian, the carnivores on either side of me always feign interest. 'I don't eat red meat' is their usual form of bonding. 'Yeah, it's probably best if you cook it first.'

The trouble with these sit-down occasions is getting stuck beside someone who is boring. Whereas normally you can make the excuse of saying 'I'm just going to the toilet' and disappear into the night, at a dinner party you can hardly come back and sit in somebody else's seat and start to eat their food. Our host decides to get the party going by putting on her Best of Funk CD, quite loud (what command of the language I have!). To me, funk is sex music and I fail to see what people sitting down at the table can get out of it. That thud of pong, ping, pong, that's not music, it's table tennis. Of course, black people do this music best and being white, the first funk you get to hear is the sanitized sounds of white funk, namely, Level 42. They put me off this music for life, much like UB40 with reggae. The night gathers momentum and little sub-parties occur, little scenes within scenes. The Beatles come on and of course we are all as one as we sing along to the bits we know. 'Play "Eleanor Rigby",' I request, only to be told that that's what's on. It was very embarrassing, I'm sure there's a French expression for it. It did give me a chance to tell my Linda McCartney story though. I'll spare you the details, but the result of our encounter was my freezer being filled with free Linda McCartney foods.

I found it nice to mingle in polite company but there lies the problem. Even though it was one o'clock by the time I got home, I felt the evening was just beginning. I decided to call it a night, however, when I discovered that the TV programme I had tried to tape hadn't come out. Actually, it was the last in the *Sean's Shorts* series. I know I've seen it before, but I have a fierce loyalty to myself. I unplug all my electricals, tip the voice-over actor and bid him goodnight.

# Waiting for the Dentist

This year I have decided to give my body an MOT. Admittedly, the multi-gym I bought six months ago has become a clothes line. So I have decided to start with the core to all one's health problems – the mouth, the place that doctors look to as a barometer for the well-being of the rest of your body, and where many an agitated female ends an argument with a good slapping. It is time for my twice-yearly dental check-up – officially that is, the reality is the once-every-five-years check-up. I'm not frightened of dentists, the sharp instruments they use I'm not too keen on though. The dentists themselves are a jolly bunch of people regardless of the fact that statistically their profession has the highest suicide rate.

I picked a new dentist in my endless search to find one who can offer treatment that doesn't involve pain, but she was much like the others I have experienced: outwardly concerned, with numbing syringe hidden behind back and a tendency to treat you like a five-year-old. Again, this isn't strictly true because my parents have never once before inflicting pain on me said, 'This will hurt a little but just let me know when and I'll stop.' Rather than the pain, I would prefer it if the dentist allowed you to stop them during one of their pointless anecdotes which for some reason they think is comforting you. I personally don't mind the pain. I am balanced enough to know it is for my own good. But even when I was five I found dentists patronizing. In my youth I fell off a push bike in gale force winds and by a strange injunction, I landed on my teeth, an angle which I'm sure would baffle even Einstein. My tooth fell out but the nerve remained alive and boy, was it pissed off. I was rushed to hospital and in emergency treatment was given a silver cap, but the one memory that stays with me until this day is, on my departure, the dentist saying in a calm and assuring way, 'And if anyone asks you how you got this, tell them you know the six million dollar man.' (It is strange how they never repeated that series. I suppose if kids saw it in these highly inflationary times they would assume it was about a second division football player.)

Of course when registering with a new dentist you have to

fill out a questionnaire. It is always at this point that I can't for the life of me remember whether or not I am allergic to penicillin. It was a first for me when she asked if I took steroids. 'Yeah,' I replied, 'but they are not working too well.' She prescribed antibiotics, and asked would I be able to stay off booze for three days? No problem, I thought, until I found out she meant consecutively. I am now booked in for various treatments over the next six weeks and I must say I am looking forward to it.

Yes, it is expensive and painful but, if the truth be told, I am addicted to the mouth rinse which the dentist gives you at the end of the visit. You may laugh, as I am sure the philistines did when Robert Palmer first admitted that he was addicted to Love. But I'm serious, and for anyone else thinking of getting into this, the blue rinse is far superior to its pink competitor. I'm talking about the gorgeous clear blue liquid which caresses the tongue, swishing around your teeth, the initial coldness embodying the enamel as it oozes around your gums; oh, and the beautiful sound it makes as it plays with your mouth; the delayed spitting out of this silky substance, mingling with tiny particles of food and falling into the miniature white, spotless marble sink; repeating this heavenly process until the perfectly formed plastic beaker is empty.

I knew I was in trouble when I asked for seconds. OK, I know heroin is cheaper and I don't get to go to any self-help groups, but I will suffer alone. When my treatment is over, I will do cold turkey dreaming of the next intake, shortening the wait by eating sugary substances. I will chomp on hard-boiled sweets and pick fights in the hope of chipping a tooth. And you may ask, 'But Sean, can't you simply buy this liquid and gargle at home to your heart's content?' And I will say to you, 'Call me Mr Hughes, because we don't know each other that well.' I have tried this unusual delight at home but it doesn't work, and it is blatantly obvious why. It is because the sensation isn't that great, but as you swill in the surgery it also signifies the end of the session, the end of the pain – the ordeal is over. The blue liquid is the lap of honour, the champagne spraying moment, the tender goodnight kiss. It is a strange addiction, I know, but at least I have admitted to it, which is the first crucial step to recovery. And it is also one of the few addictions that is actually good for your teeth.

# Bill Hicks

Life lets us know
we are gatecrashers
to a party we didn't want to be at
allowed in
we don't mingle
you give yourself
only to be spat on
you are destined to be talked about
rather than to
familiar with death
and the hereafter
the herenow being the battle
it has ended.
You win
You fucker.
Party in peace

# An Eating Experience with a Former Leader of the Opposition

The driver asked, 'Have you got a meeting with that Neil Kinnock?' I said, 'Yeah, we're plotting to bring down the government.' Without a flicker he replies, 'About time.' A free lunch from the *Express*; a rarity which I was determined to make good use of by not eating for three days beforehand. I had prepared twenty-five questions to ask Mr Kinnock. I know how tedious interviews can be and was determined not to ask him the questions that get put to him all the time. 'How did you start in politics?' was not on the agenda. The first time I met Neil Kinnock was at the Comedy Awards in November '92. He had just stepped down after losing the general election, but with the applause that greeted him, this was hard to believe. Kinnock has never been more popular than now. This is not surprising as the British public like their bigwigs more when they have been taken down a peg or two. And of course you have to remember that the television community veers to the left – the extent depending on the amount of wine consumed.

We are photographed before lunch, and we use the time to chit-chat, rumour-mongering as to who will be the next Tory stabbed in the Back to Basics. We sit down for lunch; me posing as a journalist, armed with notebook, pen and dictaphone, while he takes the role of elder statesman. Earlier today, Brian Gould resigned. Neil had only just found out about it this morning, leaving him to think on his feet without the help of the rehearsed pittle-pattle political speak we have all become accustomed to. This was the side I was trying to prise out of him today: the spontaneous Neil, relaxed over a glass of wine. But alas he was forever the diplomat, and I couldn't but notice that a lot of his words ended with a 'tion'.

He was very quotable in the sense that his answers were well thought out; intelligent but predictable. When I asked if he could speak more freely now he wasn't in the driving seat, he offered, 'I can afford to employ a lightness in my expression which I could not when I was leader.' A simple 'yes' would have done.

He reckons Labour's manifesto is identical to his own, and while he was in charge, he tried to push socialism into the '90s – much to the annoyance of the extreme Left. His views on *Socialist Worker* are that they are totally unrealistic and the question they should ask is who are they helping? The same, I think, could be said of the Labour Party.

He is trying to alleviate the Vox Populi blinkered fears of socialism with more up-to-date policies including the removal of Clause 4, which he thinks was ideal for 1918 but not an indefinite pearl of wisdom. Some people's view of socialism is that it evens things down; Neil reckons it evens things up. I commented that these were only pretty words. He replied with a stern 'in politics, words kill'. As he said it, his face seemed to reveal a thousand agonized memories.

So, Neil, what was your biggest mistake? 'Becoming leader,' he half-joked, but after some thought said, 'It was Easter '84' when he feels he should have asked the miners to have a single vote ballot. If this had happened, history would have been re-written and the pits would have been saved. He reasoned, 'Whether they striked or not, they would have been stronger and the country would have backed their solidarity. Instead the Tories couldn't believe their luck when Scargill played straight into their hands, enabling the media to put across a complete lie that the mines were to stay open, regardless of conditions or losses.' It is no secret that the newspapers in this country are biased towards the right, Neil feels they are a problem for democracy. They determine who is going to run things by offering the opinions of a tiny proportion of the public.

I asked if any written word had ever hurt him. 'Hurt is an over-statement, it is more an irritation.' The press sometimes try to pigeon-hole him as the boy from the valley, who sings at rugby matches; a part of him he is very proud of. 'Islwyn comes first,' he said as he jumped on the table and started singing 'Calon Lan'. Well, that is a slight exaggeration, but this is for the *Daily Express*. He is keen to assert his intellectual side.

He is quick, perhaps a little too quick, to emphasize how often he goes to the theatre.

It is understandable, yet unnecessary that he has to prove himself as the balanced person he obviously is. The snobbery of it all gets to him, and his sound-bite for this occasion was 'The limitation of their view damages me, but it demeans them.'

As the menu arrives, he has misplaced his glasses, and in the relaxed atmosphere he makes his first blunder, stating that British soap stars are good actors. Glenys is a big *Brookside* fan, and Neil is a passive watcher.

We chat about the Sheffield rally before the general election. He has mixed feelings as he recounts the embarrassment of the shadow cabinet coming from the back of the hall with spotlights on them. 'It was like Nuremberg,' he apologizes, while I secretly take note of this idea for the lighting of my new stage show.

I personally feel that the way forward for democracy is to involve the voters more, starting in local government. He agrees and talks of the importance of the community, in local action, and in the need for self-determination. He would like to see the equalization of local taxes, and to take the mystique out of decision-making. When the government talks about vague sums of billions, your normal voter feels out of his depth and lets them get on with it, without questioning where exactly the money is going. I would like to see the expense accounts of every politician the next time they start talking about cut-backs. Your local MP can fly to Brussels first-class and stay in a five-star hotel, or we can keep the local library open. The choice is yours – or should be.

The only slight disagreement during lunch was over censorship. Neil says he is not for censorship, but, wait for it, 'would like to secure restraint without the confines of absolute freedom'. Sounds like censorship to me.

He objects to us seeing violence implanted as normal. He has seen a bit of a video nasty and it turned his stomach. Of course I agree that children should not have access to violent films, but it is a very grey area. The government are using the copy-cat killing argument as an excuse to ban violence from television. You could use the same argument to allow a TV channel to show violence twenty-four hours a day, the theory being that these nutters would never leave the house.

At this point one of my life's ambitions was realized when a leading politician told me something off the record. I felt kind of grown-up.

I have always respected Mr Kinnock; he is a bright, caring man with well-formed opinions. He has gone up further in my estimation since our meeting, but I cannot help feeling I met Neil the politician, rather than Neil, a guy I had lunch with.

I will leave you with some more sound-bites that an off-guard Kinnock would never say but which at the same time would make great T-shirt slogans: 'the good thing about history is you're dead when it is written'; 'when you are elected you must try to leave it better than you found it'; 'if you want to look after yourself, look after somebody else'; 'you put on the badge, you have to make the decisions'.

I left the restaurant feeling pleased that he had shared some private thoughts with me, only to feel jilted seeing him later that day speaking on the news.

# A Month of Consumerism

Skirting through my end of month bank balance I notice a dip in my savings. I'm an impulsive buyer, so it takes me ages to match the payments against the goods I've bought. What the hell cost £124 from John Lewis on 6 June? I have to scour my house looking for newish things before I ring up the police to report that some cunning thief has taken my credit card and popped down to said shop before returning my card unnoticed. This happens every month. The worst is when in a drunken stupor you treat your friends to a meal, only to have no recollection of ever being at Joe's Diner in your life. The statement says otherwise. We are the credit card nation, we're led to believe it makes shopping easier – you want something, hand in the card and it's yours. This is their ploy for you to continually borrow money from them at extortionate rates of interest. The police are in on this as well, making you too paranoid to carry cash. We are sucked into using cards, while the value of money is only heeded once a month.

A chess-board and pieces, that's what cost me £124. Gordon Bennett! I spent ONE HUNDRED AND TWENTY-FOUR POUNDS on a bleeding chess-board. I somehow think if I'd paid in cash this chess-board wouldn't be gathering dust on a shelf right now, or maybe I bought an expensive set in the hope that every move I made I would cherish, psychologically gaining the upper hand on my opponent. Do I move my rook or my bishop? – be careful, each piece costs a tenner. Make it count. I played my first game of chess when I was eleven. My opponent kept on commenting on how good a player I was, that was until my first piece was captured – then I fell to pieces. Up until that moment I had been copying his every move, not actually knowing how to play. I took an interest in chess during the 1994 championship, much like people who play tennis after Wimbledon is over, only to wonder why the courts are so packed.

During snooker's heyday I took the game up. I remember entering my first snooker hall, being taken in by the serene atmosphere. The tables were bigger than expected, and the fluorescent light gave me a headache, but I was happy to be in this nether world. I went over to the cue rack and picked up what I later realized was an extension cue. This didn't seem too strange as people had said the game wasn't as easy as it looked on TV. I was told to break and off I ran towards the table with what felt like a pole vault. I missed the ball completely. I was gutted. It has to be pointed out that I'm a dreamer and when I take up something new I expect with patience and hard work to become world champion. Unfortunately after my first shot the owner of the club banned me for life. Anyway I look stupid in a waistcoat.

It was with this same dream I took up chess. It's a masterful game using the linear and lateral parts of the brain. I believe Kasparov looks fifteen moves ahead, I'm still figuring out where the pieces go on the board. It is assumed the person who invented chess was a genius, I reckon he was stoned. 'Yeah, and then you move the horsy thing, hmmph, that can move in an L-shape.' Being a pacifist I play a very defensive game and my opponents get annoyed when after they take a piece I retort, 'And what harm did he ever do you?'

My next purchase was to have cable television installed. When asked, I always say I don't watch much television, yet anytime a programme is mentioned in conversation I seem to know all about it. Maybe I should say I watch a lot of television, I just don't enjoy it much. I now have twenty-eight channels to moan about. The man who came to install it recognized me. He said, 'You're that guy from the telly aren't you?' 'I thought *you* were,' I replied. 'Nigel innit?' he said, engaging me. 'That's right, yes, I do a thing called *Nigel's Show* on Channel 4.' How good is cable? Well, basically it's shite. You have two German stations which seem to be continually showing badly dubbed *Little House on the Prairies*, MTV, which seems to be an Aerosmith theme station, and UK Gold, which shows old, not classic, editions of *Eastenders* and *Neighbours*, where the only kink value is seeing the unbelievable amount of spots the guy playing Ian Beale once had. Thanks to cable I now know what hell is: it's the remote control getting stuck on the 24-hour country and western channel.

The next big pay-out was when a friend decided we should go to Royal Ascot. I have no interest in horse racing but it was a day out in the sun, a chance to wear my suit and an opportunity to follow that grand old Irish tradition of looking the other way when the Queen appeared. The gambling system I decided to use on the day was to only pick horses whose names I could pronounce . . . suffice to say I ended up penniless after watching every race in the overcrowded bar of the grandstand.

My final purchase was to be a multi-gym, purely for light work-outs as I feel at twenty-eight this is my last attempt to be relatively healthy. Besides the health implications this has already improved my vocabulary – Trapezius, Lastissimus Dorsi, Pectoralis Major and Deltoid are all muscles I apparently have. The brochure has pictures of a couple working out, which is a bit off-putting as they look like the kind who appear in soft porn movies, the ones who during sex say things like, 'Are you really a tennis coach?' The idea is if you work out for thirty minutes a day you will notice a considerable difference. They don't seem to take into account that when I work out for twenty minutes this means spending the next four days in bed with various sprains. The guy who came to install it, George, didn't seem to have a clue what he was doing, and I was a bit worried when he left screws and odds and ends on the floor saying that they weren't important. I pointed to the brochure where it warns of possible danger of serious injury from falling weights or other moving parts. His reply was, 'You're that guy from *Sean's Show* aren't you?' I retorted with a modest 'Yes'. 'What's your name?' he asked. 'Nigel,' I replied. I'll be paying for things on a cash basis this month.

# Don't Make a Hash of It

Students seem to have been the butt of various jokes over the years, including a few from me no doubt. The stereotyping is, of course, ridiculous considering the wide net of backgrounds and personalities which we unfairly cram into the term 'student'. Realistically, if you were to do a poll of any hundred people, at least 70 per cent would turn out to be assholes, so why pick on students?

Our unimaginative media have two conflicting images of student life. One is a dashing young fellow at Oxford debating in a tuxedo, and the other is the four scruffy Levellers fans demonstrating up some tree over the latest worthy cause. *The Young Ones* showed us a caricature of four hopeless losers, but unfortunately if something captures the public's attention it tends to stick. It's the same situation that makes the public assume that all teachers wear leather patches on their elbows. Steve Coogan's character, Paul Calf – 'hit me with your dissertation' – is the latest student hater. This time we're not laughing at his student baiting, we're laughing at the crass stupidity of a character who we all know exists. It's odd that American students are deemed these hard-working young dudes, whereas in England they're shown as a bunch of piss-heads.

I was wondering why students are always given the tag of being lazy layabouts. I questioned a friend and former student and he conceded that it was because they *are* lazy layabouts. Is this such a surprise? You become a student when you are around eighteen years old. Isn't that the age when you become a lazy layabout regardless? After leaving school everybody needs those couple of years to just hang out and contemplate their future, so why not do this at university?

Is student life all that easy? Do students spend all their time going out and getting drunk? I've stayed in student accommodation and can understand their need. The college system is set up for people to further their education in the hope that they will become the future's *crème de la crème*.

Those with the best grades should go on to the best jobs. Student life is harder now that the grant system is fading out. I suppose the government's thinking is that it will encourage only the most eager and determined of people, or is something more sinister going on: a general siphoning process enabling only monied families to send their children to college? If you are ambitious, it is wise to follow in the steps of the American president – if, God forbid, you are offered a hash cake, don't swallow.

So you're a student and regardless of PR you're stuck with a bad reputation. No matter what good work is done you'll have to face facts – every time a student pops up on *The Word*, it puts your cause back fifty years. The thing to do is not to worry about your reputation. Let's face it, you're in a new town, a place where nobody knows your old nickname, it's your chance to give yourself a set of new characteristics, you can lose the ones you weren't too happy with.

You have arrived in this new town – you wanted Manchester but you're in Plymouth. On the first couple of days you don't know anyone so you'll hang out in the common room and desperately cling to anyone who will talk to you. Don't be too hasty. These are the very people you'll spend the rest of the year trying to get rid of. If the Student Union has kindly laid on a disco for you, try to resist the temptation of sitting on the dance floor when the DJ plays 'Sit Down' by James. This is a song, not a command. Don't get too impressed by the second and third year students who end up getting off with the good-looking first years. You will come to realize in your second year that it's only morons who go to the freshers' disco. Please do remember to study, don't leave it to the last minute and pressurize yourself. The university can do without those suicide statistics. Try to make your study period clash with *Going for Gold*, *This Morning* and *Pebble Mill*. If my future lies in your hands I don't want you watching these programmes. It's the first step on the way to becoming one of those letter-writing, 'Agitated from Plymouth' types.

On the other hand, do try to watch *Fifteen to One*, as this will give you a good indication as to what kind of grade you will get. If you manage to get over two questions right over the series, you shouldn't have any problems. If, like me, you don't listen to the questions but you just choose a contestant in the hope that they'll win, you're probably better off dropping out right now. By the way the very first thing you should do is change the subject you have picked: Chemistry might have seemed a good idea when filling out your form, but the reality of having to actually study it every day is a terrifying one. Join that queue trying to get on to some media-related course. And try to befriend a medical student – it's handy after a night out on a binge.

# A Mapped-out Walk

Being pushed forward
two prams collide
offering a diversion
the hand-held couple cause the delay
the arrogance of muscle trips you up
the free-thinker helps you on your way
a colourful window display welcomes a break
a tramp's distress moves you enough to stop
a street gang quickens your step
a friendly dog becomes a beautiful distraction
a charity worker gives peace of mind
a car crash screeches somebody's life to a halt
the crowd gathers round
I take a side street.

# Titanic Motives

'More by luck than judgement, here am I.' So goes one of Julian Cope's theories on life. A fifteen-year career span has seen him in many guises. Fifteen years of being a fan has seen me in many guises. The remarkable thing being I love him now more than ever. Usually what happens is somebody will come along at just the right time and say all the things you wanted to say, you share the moment but slowly drift apart. I somehow don't think that if the Bay City Rollers were still going strong I'd share the same enthusiasm for their next release, and yet at the time I would have killed for them or at the very least supplied the weapons. Julian Cope is destined, probably in death, to be given his place in the hall of fame. As far as the media is concerned he has been in and out of favour continually, never really put up on a pedestal, more given a soft spot in most comprehensive record collections. And why is that so? Music is oft written about, a band is championed in the weeklies, given space in the monthlies and becomes mass culture when the qualities eventually pick up on it. The problem being, the tired and trying media are continually looking for new trends, even going to the extent of making one up if the situation calls for it. It seems to be you get your one chance to shine before being relegated to the 'we've heard that before' section. On the other hand, a band with one song and the right image is given preference. I find the short-sightedness frightening. I don't understand why, in a culture that has so little quality, the media still feels the need to dish it up, chew it about and spit it back out so quickly. Where the great often go unnoticed, 'Oasis Go Shopping' may soon be worthy of a front cover – laugh, Morrissey got one for signing some autographs.

This is the inherent problem of music journalism. The writers are obsessed by music, they feel a compulsion to write about it, start to earn a living from it, it becomes a job, they rub shoulders with pop stars. The magic goes. It stands to reason: the kid waiting eight months for OMD to come to Dublin, or the person making the last-minute phone call to be added to the guest list – who's the most excited? I suppose the one with the gram of speed in their pocket.

I've always had a massive appreciation of music, it's

probably too important to me. Julian Cope stands for every-thing good about music – ever moving, continually chal-lenging, in short a visionary. In interviews I'm often asked that same question, 'Did you really want to become a pop star?' The answer is always no. I love music too much – anyway after years of playing the air guitar I found I never improved. On three occasions I even went as far as trying to learn to play the real thing. It takes perseverence, time and hard skin on your finger-tips. I figure anyone can learn guitar, with the possible exception of Sid Vicious. I'm not saying anyone can become a virtuoso, but the basics can be grasped at. What stopped me? I wanted to retain that mystery, to see somebody on stage making beautiful sounds from such a simple instrument without having to think that was A followed by C minor bridging to an E.

The first band I really adored was the Bay City Rollers. Me and a bunch of girls would go all woozy at the very mention of Woody. My next obsession, unfortunately, was Gillan. Thankfully, this only lasted six days. At the time every drain-piped jeans-wearing macho man was into heavy metal. Every Friday night was spent trying to make our hair look longer and then strut-ting down to the local disco, forming a circle and head banging the night away. Thinking about it now, I haven't been able to dance in public since.

The Sex Pistols came along at just the right time. I bought 'God Save the Queen' without ever hearing it. There wasn't much option, as our local radio stations had smoochy songs on heavy rotation. 'This one goes out to Tomo, Zem, Jocko, Mayhem and The Clontarf Posse. Here's Chicago.' I embraced punk fully, I even had two Crass singles imported from England. Like most punks I had more badges than records. If the truth be told, I was a little short in the tooth for punk and it was only when Dexy's Midnight Runners came along that I could sigh with relief. At last a band I could call my own whose very conception I was there for. 'Searching for the Young Soul Rebels' was released, and out we went searching.

A cliché usually comes into play at this point, the one that goes 'it became the soundtrack to my life', but it wasn't, it was the soundtrack to Kevin Rowland's life. This was the first time I became aware of the fact that you could like more than one style of music. You didn't have to be just a Mod or just a New Romantic. I more or less liked everything, which showed in my appalling dress sense. Around this time, I was aware of two cracking tunes – 'Treason' and 'Reward' from a band called the Teardrop Explodes. I also knew the singer wore a ridiculous flying jacket and had a way-out haircut. During this period I found music liberating and I used to hang out at second-hand record shops constantly looking for bargains. On one such occasion, 14 September 1983, I bought 'Wilder' by The Teardrop Explodes and a record by a band called After The Fire for a fiver. After one play the After The Fire record was put in the section I called 'Dodgy Mistakes'. I was initially disappointed with 'Wilder' when I noticed the singles weren't on it, but I was intrigued by the sleeve notes. The album is a classic. The Teardrop Explodes were a pop group, and being a naïve seventeen-year-old I saw album tracks as songs not good enough to be singles. 'Wilder' blew this theory to bits as every track was bliss to my ears and all other living segments of my body. I was beginning to doubt whether the best-selling songs were actually the best. Obvious maybe, but an insight to me. With 'Wilder' I was haunted by the sadness of it arriving in a second-hand shop; the idea that somebody had heard it and then decided to sell it mortified me.

Julian was my spring-board into what music could mean. I gobbled up the first Teardrops album, 'Kilimanjaro', and although it contained the two aforementioned singles I still preferred 'Wilder'. What's that they say about first love? I soon started collecting any Teardrops stuff the shops could throw at me, I even had the French version of 'Treason'. This was the wrong time to start following Julian, as he had just split up the band and was in hiding. Nevertheless, I busied myself with all the tit-tat that goes on between releases. I found that one of the unwritten laws of the era was that if you liked the Teardrops you weren't allowed to like Echo and the Bunnymen, although secretly we all liked both bands. The 'all' being me and my mate, as my local area was still witnessing a frenzied obsession with heavy metal.

As the boundaries of my life stretched over the thousand metre mark which was my existence, I found other Cope devotees. This was strange in itself, as Julian has what can only be described as the most English of accents. Not the most popular accent to the youth of Ireland who were reading history at school every day, which went something like – Page 1: The English came over, raped, pillaged and murdered the Irish. Page 2: See page 1. On top of this, Julian had a habit of singing in a very whimsical, nursery rhyme style. I had this vision of a Republican march going through Dublin shouting 'Brits Out' – with ten of us at the back holding banners, stating 'Except Julian'.

Awaiting the next release, I would spend time studying the lyrics deeper. Where others often wonder what their heroes are like in real life, I was always happy just to hear his output. Why spoil the magic? Julian's lyrics, although never simple, have this terrible habit of popping into my head at any given time to make sense of a situation. The line that kept recurring then was 'Secret dreams of Melanie and Melanie knows who I mean'. Unfortunately I took this to be a starting gun for me to start writing the most incomprehensible poetry I could muster. These were the kind of poems you show to a few baffled friends, explaining them word by word, waiting to be crowned a genius. Julian's lyrics have always puzzled me, but you always get a general feeling that you're in safe hands. On the first track I heard – 'Passionate Friend' – there is the line 'Celebrate the great escape and carry my soul away'. On reflection, this was probably about the divorce he was going through, but to me it was about the discovery of this music. Anyway, it beats 'I want to move it, move it' every time.

At this stage of his career he was taking his pop star hat off and trying on assorted others. This was a risk, as I doubt he was aware how good he could be. So out faded the Teardrops, losing the fame with the hope of gaining the recognition. He probably realized he was too intelligent to battle for the pop stakes and there wasn't much chance with that haircut. He decided to traipse off into the unknown alone, not knowing there were a lot of us out there ready to man the barricades for him.

These pieces always give the false impression that if you are obsessed by a band you spend every minute of your life thinking about them. This is not the case, but nostalgia will always heighten the tiny moments. Music is there essentially for us to relax to, to enjoy, to – dare I say – make us happy, but at its most powerful it's there to relate to.

When you meet someone new you try to find common ground. We also do this through music. If somebody likes the same music as you there's a fair chance that you'll be on the same wavelength. How many times have you heard a song, wishing that the person you loved was listening to it with you, and that the pair of you could claim the sentiment behind the lyric as yours? Inevitably this thought only occurs when alone. Music is best listened to by oneself; when with others you're always too conscious of whether they're enjoying it or not. One of the worst feelings is when you play something to a friend which you think is awe-inspiring, only to be told to turn it down. The best discoveries are always found alone, you can't force your taste on others. Mind you, it doesn't stop me trying. I would love to strap people into a chair and make them listen to Julian's entire back catalogue. They'd thank me for it eventually.

It never rains, it pours, and out I ran into the drizzle when I heard he was playing a gig in Dublin. He was here to plug his first solo album, 'World Shut Your Mouth'. For some reason the record stores didn't share my enthusiasm, and it was only with the concert a day away that I managed to track it down. I couldn't understand why it hadn't made the national news: 'Julian Cope's album is available in Freebird'. But there it was, and on the cover Julian had surpassed himself on the hair front.

With the reviews it was getting I was worried, as I was still at the impressionable age where I believed what reviewers wrote. I got home and played it sixty times. I had this system for listening to new records. The first time I'd try to get a general feel for it, while coping with the anxiety that my crap record player would give me with its tendency to skip and scratch. The second airing was with lyric sheet in front of me, sussing out the content. After ten plays one song usually stands out, and I'd play that continually for an hour. I loved the album, but it did seem the work of a man fighting his corner; not so much depressing, more a man in isolation. At times it gave me the creeps.

At the gig itself I figured I knew the album better than Julian himself. I was walking around, cocksure, name-dropping tracks from the album. 'I hope he does "Pussy Face". Oh, you've not heard it yet?' I know it was an asshole thing to do but this was my night. It got to the extent I felt nobody was allowed to enjoy the gig as much as me, and I demanded they give full concentration while he was on. I was probably too nervous to really enjoy it, much like a parent watching their child on stage for the first time. He eventually appeared after midnight. He was probably having a ball backstage. I still don't understand why groups keep us waiting. I can just picture the scenario in the dressing-room. 'Are you ready?' 'Yeah.' 'Okay, give it another half an hour.' I'd heard many bootlegs of Julian live and I knew he was keen to interact with an audience. It was a bit of an anticlimax when he walked on in a white shirt and went straight into 'The Greatest Imperfection Is Love'. He'd finish a song, put down the guitar and walk over to the piano and start the next one. There were others in the audience trying to impress Julian as well, as people started calling out for B sides. This became the game for the night. The more obscure the song, the more brownie points awarded. I won hands down when I started making them up. 'Do "Titanic Motives",' I'd shout with my knowing look. It wasn't a great show, he seemed troubled, but I was satisfied and anyway we were at that stage of the relationship where anything was forgivable. The second I got home I played the album again recollecting the live versions of the songs.

A week later in London he ripped his stomach open during 'Reynard the Fox'. I thought that was the beginning of the end.

We only had to wait another eight months for 'Fried' to appear, he was spoiling us. This was an album worth growing your hair for. There he was on the cover again, this time photographed under a turtle shell while his contemporaries donned shell suits for their covers. This came as no surprise to me, but of course the thoughtless media picked up on Mad Julian. I don't understand this, when all it was was a man expressing himself without fear of what others would think. On the strength of the cover I expected him to be at his most experimental, and I put it on the turntable with some trepidation. There was always that worry that he had gone too far the other way and it would become one of those albums that you say you like but you rarely play. Does 'My Bloody Valentine' ring a bell? Yes, there were some very introspective songs but in the main it was tunes, tunes, tunes, in fact some of my all-time favourite hummables. In the press it would be called an uneven album, meaning that there isn't a band's trademark style filling every groove. The importance of Julian can be seen in his wanting to take you on a journey where various moods are encountered. It was never going to be an easy ride. Where others musically just open the door for you, Julian lets you rummage around every room offering to let you stay the night.

In all the arts we are looking for entertainment, that is, to escape from the humdrum. But where most want to escape in a cosy, nice, let's forget our troubles sort of way, there are others who want knowledge and a gathering of new thoughts and to be taken to some scary places along the way. Julian is there for the latter. Again, it's very easy to say Julian makes very acid-indulged records. This belittles him in every sense. It's a basic requirement of any artist to view life from different angles. You never create on the drugs themselves, it's the being in various states of mind which makes you question the norm. You don't need to take drugs to be able to relate, in fact at the time I was extremely frightened of them. I don't like the feeling of being out of control, but I was glad somebody was taking those trips for me and coming back with the news.

Julian's next LP, 'Saint Julian', didn't appear for three years. I did most of my growing up during this period and music wasn't as important. I moved to London for a start, leaving behind most of my record collection bar a few tapes. I felt I'd outgrown them. Julian was like an old friend who you grow apart from as the regiment of your life changes. One day I was walking aimlessly down the tube station when I saw a guy with shades on. I thought what a prat. It was Julian. I ran up one escalator and down the other in a blind panic as this utter compulsion had me running towards him. With my heart leaping I tapped him on the shoulder with my shaky hand. 'Julian I love you, what are you up to?' He looked heavenly and he is the only person who can say 'Wow man, far out, cool' and get away with it. I feel these words were invented for his use. He told me he was doing a gig next week and had a new album coming out. London, I thought, was paved with pop icons.

The gig itself was upstairs in the Boston Arms in Tufnell Park. A little watering hole in north London. It was sold out. I was squatting with a scouser named Dave at the time, and that day was when we collected our dole. We decided to chance our arm. We arrived at the pub at three, just as it was closing, but with our bad smelling clothes and druggy eyes the barmaid mistook us for part of the group. 'Straight up those stairs, guys', and on opening up the pearly gates there was Julian dressed in leather on his now legendary mike stand doing a sound check. It was an odd feeling listening to this beautiful voice when just outside there were tramps swigging Special Brew, kebab shops offering off-cuts and single mothers walking the routed daily walk. There was beauty amid the decay. We approached his then manager Cally, and I lied that I'd come over especially from Dublin, Dave pretended he'd come from Liverpool and how he used to see them all the time at Eric's (a club that started the Liverpool scene). Cally said there was nothing he could do for us, but as we were about to leave he handed us two back-stage passes and told us we could sell T-shirts at the back of the hall. I asked Julian did he remember me from the tube station. He pretended he did, God bless him.

As the crowd came in we sold the T-shirts in a matter of minutes and suddenly we had £600 in our possession. It was very tempting just to do a bunk and we agreed if we didn't like the first three songs we'd do a runner. Julian came on unaware he was singing for his supper. It was breathtaking and after the three songs we split with the money – only joking. We kept on smiling inanely at each other all night, pinching each other in disbelief, our enjoyment enhanced by the fact that we felt part of the team. Cally took the money and offered us his thanks. We were having none of it. It was back to the hotel for us, transported there in a little minibus, sitting next to Julian no less. Of course, none of our friends believed us, but it somehow didn't matter.

'Trampoline' and 'World Shut Your Mouth' had Julian playing the pop star once again. This couldn't last long. All of a sudden everyone was excited and I remember one review of 'World Shut Your Mouth' going as far as to say that one day this would become a football anthem. I'm afraid to report that down at the Palace they still favour 'Glad All Over'. It was with a certain pride that we saw Julian back in the charts, but it felt uncomfortable rubbing shoulders with fourteen-year-old girls again.

Album, tour, album, tour has never really suited Julian but he played along with it. Unfortunately the rigours of time and success brought about his weakest album, 'My Nation Underground', the following year. Julian was never going to be number 1, and to play in the pop arena he'd have to work harder than most. To sell tickets and records you have to do a lot of publicity, and if you are continually asked the same questions by people who don't really care, it becomes very frustrating. With 'My Nation Underground' there is a feeling of Julian wanting both worlds. It was a concept album without the concept. As a loyal fan I bought the record and went to the concert but felt he was passing me by. It was depressing thinking he was losing it. The only shining light coming from the confusion was 'Charlotte Anne', which can only be described as a Julian Cope song.

I wasn't to know that a new cycle was appearing, two stabs at the pop world and two fingers up to it. But maybe the album title was prophetic as he went underground again. I thought he might do a Syd Barrett and spend the rest of his days playing with his Dinky toys at the back of the garden. 1990 saw two official bootlegs, 'Droolian' and 'Skellington', both extremely extreme but of course containing gems like 'Jelly Pop Perky Jean' which I had the good fortune to have a bash at on *Sean's Show*. I was delighted to hear he liked it and had it on tape.

'Peggy Suicide' appeared, much like the corn circles, in March 1991, and to say he had reinvented himself is again to belittle his genius because this is what he was aiming for from day one. The sleeve notes themselves were worth the price of the record alone. Where 'My Nation Underground' let you know you could go through a dull patch and come out the other end, 'Peggy Suicide' made you aware of what we are all capable of. This went beyond fandom; after fifteen years he'd been hiding this from us, the cheeky pup. When you talk of the great songwriters, Lennon and McCartney, Richards and Jagger, Morrissey and Marr, this was Cope and Cope. The musicianship had never been stronger. This will go down as one of the all-time great records, it's the sort of album that aliens will land for. I thought this is it, this can't be surpassed. Then in 1992 he released 'Jehovah Kill'. This is the sort of record aliens did land for and helped out with in the studio no doubt. This is the masterpiece that Island Records dropped him over. He might have been disappointed but I was delighted. Never again would he play at being a pop star. You can keep your record industry, we want Julian to ourselves, we'll pay the wages.

The reason for writing this is to get across the importance of music, the importance of being a fan. When we go through our record collection it's the newest ones we rush to play, but it's those records like Julian's that you go back to time and again. It's not that Julian is unknown – he has been praised – but when the media praise him there's always that footnote: he's mad, you know.

I'll accept that, if madness means not being frightened, not frightened to grow, of wearing his weaknesses, showing us his loves, his new discoveries, but most importantly not being frightened of being frightened. I'll go along with that, in fact I want to be certified now. It should also be pointed out that this madman is happily married with two children.

The importance of Julian Cope to me can never be over-stated. As a teenager you want music to hit you in the face. In your early twenties you want a more thoughtful groove, and as you turn twenty-nine you want an intelligent, fulfilling sound to accompany you as you walk your dog. For any person to influence even a tiny part of your life they should be bowed to, for somebody to continually excite you throughout your various states of mind is mystifying. I've met Julian on many occasions, but I like to keep it to a quick hello – I feel no need to bore him with my chit-chat. I respect the man too much. Let's just be happy he exists and thank God that he still has the ego to keep on sharing his thoughts with us.

# Ooh Ah Vince Hilaire!

The very idea of sex as performance has me hiding under my bed, not for the motive of finding a new position, more for fear of being caught short. As a teen you're told to try and make sex last as long as possible. 'Think of footballers,' I was told. Every time I found myself in bed with a lover I was straining to remember the Crystal Palace first eleven. 'Who's Vince Hilaire?' she'd ask. This has worked to varying degrees: sometimes I could make sex last up to forty minutes. Mind you, that was including the bus journey to her house. I'm not complaining, the ones I feel sorry for are the actual footballers. Who are they supposed to think of?

My first sexual experience was hearing my parents making love. Fortunately, I didn't have your liberal 'Sean, come quickly, your Dad's about to orgasm' types. Mine tried to protect me from such traumas by telling me I had to wear ear-mufflers in bed. 'Honestly, son, it keeps the bed bugs at bay.' Ever fearful of being caught out, they kept noise to a minimum.

On losing my virginity I was rather startled by the strange howling my partner was making. I panicked and rang 999. One irate ambulance driver later, I realized this was par for the course. It is important not to be too self-conscious. In essence, good sex only happens when you lose yourself in it, and it's better not to rate the performance afterwards. Once I lit the cigarette and said, 'You were great' and she shouted, 'Put it in now, Sean.'

There are certain mood enhancers like sexy movies, music and perfumes – which is odd since men seem to be continually horny anyway. The point is, sex is always a gamble, and sometimes the mere suggestion of it has me spent. Other times it goes on for so long I need a cigarette break. Alcohol and responsibility are the main adversaries to good sex. The act itself is all about fantasy, and I would recommend never living any of them out. In your mind, doing it doggy fashion in a train toilet is fun. In reality, the erratic movement, your arse cramped up against the sink, the tap that won't stop running and the smell of urine will have you wishing you were in a cosy bed in the missionary position.

I was brought up a romantic, the only concession to these grim times being that I am now a romantic realist. We all see images of the two beautiful healthy 20-somewhats toying with each other's designer under-garments, trying every concoction of body wrapping, then congratulating themselves after three hours of non-sweating, non-stop, vigorous sex.

They awake in the morning, wash off the remains of the Haagen-Dazs and promise to fax each other. How are we mere mortals supposed to cope with that? If we thought of ourselves in bed, we'd all be celibate. I sometimes get accused of being a sex symbol. So think of being in bed with this skinny 9-stoner, trying to hide my funkless underpants, only changing the position when part of my body has gone numb or to check if I've cracked a rib – and when it's all over, none of those sweet nothings, just the argument as to who has to wipe it off.

When it comes to how good sex can be, it doesn't really matter what state of mind you're in or how much preparation has gone on, it is and always will be about the chemistry between two people – or six (if you're open-minded). Personally, the best performance is given when unexpected, and I don't mean the nonsense you read on the problem pages. You know the sort of thing: 'I was just sitting on the bus and this woman came over and sat on my face. I nearly crashed and lost my job.' More, the unexpected sex where you're in a relationship and you've had a wonderful night out – later you're in bed and you remember why you fancy each other and you express this through love-making. This is not to be confused with sex. That's just something you do in the morning as a kick-start before breakfast. The more we forget about love-making as a fulfilling experience, the less we remember that sex is an empty one. A pleasant one, I know, but too self-gratifying and deceiving. Modern sex is press-ups for the generation frightened to go to the gym on their own. Having said that, the only time I have ever multi-orgasmed was when I was taken to my first game at Crystal Palace. 'Vince Hilaire,' I moaned as I was ejected from the ground.

# Shade

It's a feeble heart
that tries to whimper to you
and I find myself drunk
staring at the lost bodies
trying to cuddle up to a piece of you
a touch to bring about rest
excuses, excuses and I want to
punch myself hard about the face
to lose consciousness
wake up a different person

# Everyone a Winner

The National Lottery has at last been launched in Britain. John Major lit some fancy firecrackers, starting the dream for millions of gullible souls. Queues formed early morning, the grinning and the winking and the asides, the common link being the 'what's a pound' expression on sad people's faces. The Noel Edmunds stable of celebrities will announce the winners in colourful suits. They will be paid well to shake the sweaty-palmed winners' hands. The whole infrastructure of our lives will no doubt change. Now, every Saturday, before we make use of our weekend relaxation methods, we will check to see if we have become millionaires.

In my teens, I was a compulsive gambler. Of course, I had very little to lose, which unfortunately is always the way with compulsive gamblers. I worked part time in a supermarket and my minimum wage went straight into Playland's poker machines. I never thought I had a problem, I thought Gamblers Anonymous was when you got a friend to put the bet on for you. The poker machine was certainly my weak spot. No partic-ular skill was involved unless you call the ability to stand in front of flashing lights at eight-hour stretches a talent. I tried horse race gambling but gave up when a horse I had backed fell early on. I know this happens all the time, but this partcular race was run on a flat course. He just barged into the side railings. I stuck to the poker machines, which I still have fond memories of regardless of losing my money each time. That tremendous buzz of excitement, I can remember it as if it was yesterday. Actually, it was yesterday. To pass two minutes in a pub, I threw six quid into a slot machine, taken in by the slight palpitations, colourful lights and, wait for it, the jackpot of six quid.

There lies the rub, compulsive gamblers like gambling, the winning isn't that important, what is important is the idea that you might win. Oh, the beautiful memories of walking home, penniless, in the freezing cold as the cosy buses pass me by, running on time for once. Even then, I wouldn't dare say never again. It was always 'next time'. The following six nights would be spent indoors amusing oneself with all the things in life that are free, like shampooing my hair with the samples that are shoved through my letterbox on a regular basis. It was all worth it for those few times the fifty-pound royal flush would come up. These moments are indescribable as the King, Queen and the rest of the family flash before you. Of course I would never take my winnings, being an anti-royalist. After hearing all this, you might think I would be a likely candidate for the lottery, but true gamblers will not be participating with the odds at 14,000,000 to 1. I would get a better price if I entered my dog into the next Grand National.

With the lottery, people say, 'Isn't it only a bit of fun and isn't a lot of the money going to charity and the Arts? Everyone's a winner.' And where will most of this money be coming from? Methinks from the ones for whom a pound is still a lot of money. The problem for me is that the lottery isn't a gamble, it's another form of government tax, and by rights the next time the council tax is due you should be allowed to pay in losing lottery tickets. And where exactly is this money going? (Wait for it, Kafka fans.) It goes to what the committee deem worthy arts and charity organizations. Don't worry, conspiracy theorists, you can be assured that they will cover themselves by giving hand-outs to one or two high-profile populist organizations. But the fact of the matter is, it is a poor man's tax, there to support a rich man's pleasures. Here is an idea. How about the actual winner being allowed to pick where the profit goes to? I somehow don't think that will be in line with the government's thoughts on the matter. I'm sure the homeless are already forming queues to get a look at Churchill's letters. This is the same government that taxes gambling to discourage it. The tax on gambling can, say, help subsidize the theatre. Theoretically, I haven't got a problem with that. I think theatre should be affordable. Everybody should be able to enjoy the spectacle of seeing something that makes you think, laugh, cry, get anxious and feel like jumping up and down. That pretty much describes what my father goes through on a Saturday afternoon watching the horse racing, the *Racing Post* being his commemorative programme. It is too easy to say that gambling is taxed because it is mainly a working-class pastime, only respectable when the Queen does her each-way bet at Royal

Ascot. Some see gambling as an addiction, perhaps leading some to thieve to feed their habit, and of course you don't get that many theatre-related crimes. I am not anti the lottery *per se*, but let's not get carried away with what it really is. The only thing that surprises me is how incompetent this government is to have taken so long to get it going. By all means enjoy it. I will have fun thinking of various old people watching the draw shouting 'House' thinking it's bingo, but I for one will not be buying a ticket. But next week I would predict 12, 14, 29, 31, 36 and 49. Incidentally, Ladbrokes have just quoted me odds of 5,000 to 1 on my dog winning the National. It could be a nice each-way bet.

# It Wasn't What I Asked For

I have just come back from the swish John Frieda salon off Park Lane thirty pounds lighter and looking in the mirror, I think they charge by the individual hair. I am not really big on hair dressing (you surprise us Sean, you are usually so positive about everything). The comb is mine enemy. I don't like neat hair. The only time it has ever been combed is when I was attacked by a gang of leather-clad flick-comb maniacs. I don't like those cuts people get where they are frightened to move their face in case they ruin the desired look. I rarely shampoo my hair. Why take two bottles into the shower when you can simply dunk your hair under the bathwater? As you might have gathered, I am not that fussy about my hair. Having said that, it does take me at least eight hours to get it just right. This is called sleep. I am presently going through a long-hair phase. This is commonly known in the business as a 'this could be your last attempt at this length' look. This is a realistic fear. I have a brother a year older than me who is beginning to resemble a coot and my father lost his hair overnight, mind you, that was in a poker game.

If I may generalize wildly, the sexes have extremely different attitudes towards hairdressing. Men tend to go six times a year to one of those 'appointments not always necessary' type places while women choose the flashy sickly-smelling salons, visiting once a fortnight for one of those 'not so you'd notice' haircuts. There is a third category which is the old women who forgo eating to enable them to change the colour of their hair once a week, determined to go through every spectrum of the rainbow before they decide which colour goes best with the coffin.

I've gone through many a haircut. Some were brilliant, others disastrous, the majority have grown on me. The one thing they have all had in common is that every cut has left little hairs to run down my neck to itch my back for many days after. My earliest memory is of my Dad dragging me down to the scary Greek barbers, screaming with fear. I'd soon calm him down though. I miss that plank of wood and the wasted energy of explaining in intricate detail exactly what style I wanted only for the barber to wait for the nod from my father before inflicting on me the same haircut they gave every little boy. Then there were the times just before fashion entered my vocabulary (early twenties) when my mother would practise her complete lack of haircutting skills on me. Armed only with a kitchen knife and Tupperware bowl, her battle cry being I can do it just as well as any hairdresser, fell on deaf slightly-bleeding ears.

Her completely mystifying mathematics came into play here too as half-an-inch suddenly became four inches. My Dad stayed well out of these arguments ever since we found a bottle of Grecian 2000 hidden in his wardrobe and casually mentioned it in front of his friends.

The teenage expressive rebellious cuts came next, the ones that never quite worked out as you imagined. These are the haircuts you will always deny, the blank pages in the photo album which can't be accounted for – 'I don't know folks, I don't think we took any photos during that five-year period.' Of course there was the obligatory skinhead cut where it is only afterwards that it dawns on you that you have a head shaped like a peanut.

Then there is your first visit to a proper salon where you get to drink coffee, listen to the latest dance records and they actually wash your hair. You are in a different world, one where barbers don't exist, replaced by stylists who will tell you what suits you best. It is a strange one but have you ever seen a hairdresser with a decent haircut? And yet how would you feel if you went into an estate agents only to find it being run by a bunch of homeless people? Hairdressers have this unexplained power over you. They take control of your brain. You look into the mirror to see them making a complete hash of your hair. The need to enter every Peter Beardsley look-alike competition and the afterthought of never trusting a hairdresser situated beside a hat shop never far from your mind.

You want to kill him when it is over and he says: 'How is that?' but the only words you can muster are 'that's fine'. And then they have the cheek to show you the back. You sit there thinking there has surely been some mistake and it must be like a Rolf Harris cartoon where there will be one last fantastic stroke and it will all make sense but no, they are finished. And it is two weeks indoors for me and on the way home from such a haircut, you are guaranteed to meet every person you have ever known.

# The Illusion of Laziness

My favourite state of mind is that sleepy sensation you find yourself in late afternoon when you can nod off at any given moment. To me this is bliss, and on the occasion of my death I expect all my good deeds to go noticed and to be told that eternity will be spent in this state. Unfortunately, to reach this utopia you have to have had a busy day beforehand. I'm not a big fan of doing exercise. It bores me, yet I can watch workouts on television to my heart's content. Is this indicative of society, the fact that fitness exists in itself is enough for us? I feel the same about religion – that general feeling that if things get bad, you might turn to it one day or maybe this really says something about my own personality. Yet in my youth I was second best in my school at cross-country running. Dare I say I even enjoyed it, not the rigmarole of carrying a sports bag, changing into togs in front of strangers or wearing abysmal vests, but the actual running. Years later, I was told that during a long run your brain actually produces a natural heroin, thus giving you a high as you run. If only my teacher had told me this then I could have saved myself a lot of sweating and just gone out and scored some smack. Mind you, I did have my suspicions, as the school's best runner was a junkie going through cold turkey. I always thought it odd that he laughed uncontrollably when the starting gun was fired.

Don't get me wrong. I'm not a fan of idleness. In fact when I see those old people whose life amounts to waking up in the morning with the thought of 'nearly time for bed', I say let's legalize euthanasia. And let's not confine this to age either. Any person who spends more than eight hours on a couch watching television should also be given the big injection, unless of course they have the excuse of having a hangover – then it's perfectly understandable.

This brings me to the question of what constitutes laziness. Sadly, there will always be someone doing more than you, hence you will always be seen as lazy by certain people. You are basically left with two options. Firstly, you can do a bit more, jump on the frustrated ladder of feeling part of the pack, accepting that you are always going to be a lower-rung person. Otherwise, you could simply get out of our infra-structured work system altogether. The only good point for staying within the system is that there will always be people doing *less* than us as well. Try to meet the standards of the pop group The Stone Roses, who took five years to create their difficult second album.

I am sick of reading about writers telling us about their working day, because it always sends spasms of guilt through my system. They say they get up at 7 a.m., work until 6 p.m., have a glass of wine and get straight back into it. By stating this, they want to impress upon us that it is not a frivolous piece of work but a well-thought-out muse on life. Public relations companies tend to use such information to sell their work to us.

Realistically, you will only come up with one or two good ideas during the day, so what exactly are we being told? The writer wrote for eight hours and got two ideas out of it. Unfortunately, the editor wants seventy thousand words, so it all stays in. I am very much of the school of letting an idea come to you, inviting it in, letting it stay overnight, fondling it, then in the morning committing to it or asking it to leave. There is also the other PR angle of stating that a certain work 'took over two years to write'. Yes, it's called writer's block. Unfortunately, some writers come across this problem but continue writing regardless. They are called 'best-sellers'. It has to be said that it is of vital importance not to give work in too early. I can hardly go into Channel 4 and say, 'Here's my new show, I hope you like it, I wrote it in an hour', but in essence this is true, the fundamental idea will come in a brainstorm. The film *The Long Good Friday* was apparently written over a weekend. Sylvester Stallone wrote *Rocky* in a day. This is refreshingly arrogant and a big porky-pie. I know he's a muscle man, but I can only physically write for about two hours a day.

Although brought up Catholic, I have a tremendous Protestant work ethic, something I dare not confess to a priest, but because of this ailment, I am left with many hours to while away with pretend work. Posting a letter or emptying a waste-paper basket can take upwards of a morning, and I sometimes kid myself that watching television is research. The only way to allay my guilt is to carry a Dictaphone with me at all times. This way I am constantly on call, that includes Christmas Day. I start my working week by off-loading these thoughts to paper. Some are wonderful, others complete nonsense. If there is a lot of mumbling on tape, I know I've fallen for that age-old trick of thinking you are having great ideas when pissed. The best of this week's offerings was about those con-artists who insist on washing your windscreen without being asked. To counterbalance this, I now get out of the car and start to shampoo their hair, then demand payment. I don't think I'm lazy as I will always put in at least three hours' work a day, unless of course I get an early breakthrough, in which case I usually treat myself to a packet of Quavers or two weeks in Malta. It should be pointed out that this piece took eight years to write and was originally supposed to be of the five thousand word variety.

# Take Me Now, Lord

I'd like to thank God for fucking up my life and at the same time not existing – quite a special skill I think you'll agree.

Hopefully some of you will have taken offence at this less than innocent remark; maybe you could put a fatwa on my head, as apparently they are quite fashionable around this time of year. Thankfully I wasn't brought up under the influence of Islam, where I would be immediately assassinated. Being Catholic means the worst that could happen to me is I might get a good kicking from a bunch of farmers from Westmeath. I am an atheist. I don't say this in a rebellious, throwing a cigarette on the floor, combing my hair and donning my leather jacket sort of way. My statement comes from the well-thought-out scary revelation that when I die, it's ashes to ashes, end of story. You believers can cherish that eternal cup of coffee with Cliff Richard in Heaven. The tut-tuts might come from the elders who watch the young leave the church in droves only to come back with a vengeance when on their last legs, attending mass every day and confessing the minutiae that only people losing their faculties confess. 'Is knitting a sin, Father?' 'I'll have to check the good book, my dear.'

I have established that being an atheist is frightening, but less so than being brought up Catholic, where every late-night noise was the devil coming to get me. True, this fear has been replaced by the lost souls with severe mental problems who have been thrown into the care in the community scheme of things. Pray tell why are you sharing this with us, Sean? Aren't you antagonizing a harmless select group? I like a reader who asks questions, but my aim isn't to produce more atheists (safety in numbers) but to ask people to think why they believe in Jesus in the first place.

I know I've got hang-ups, which I hold my upbringing directly responsible for, and I'm sick of reading about the emotionally-charged individuals who vent their frustration through horrid deviant sexual acts – but it's not my place to talk about priests. I'd rather warn of the children's plight who are born into the septic '90s, born into a religion they can never live up to, having to suppress their natural evil side which – come, come – is allowable and when filtered through properly amounts to nothing more than being an asshole on occasion. I also should point out that Dana is a one-off, an angel in long skirts who, it has to be said, has had sex on a regular basis. Okay, there is that strange gene pool that went disastrously wrong re Daniel O'Donnell who by all accounts is a saint but I'm willing to put money on the fact that he masturbates on a regular basis – it isn't a sin – it's called writing a regular column in the *Sunday World*. Yes, I'll pay good money to hear his arguments on the pro-life debate among other intellectualized philosophies.

The church is redundant and missing basic points. Why not convert some churches into hostels for the homeless, or is that a bit too practical? I was an altar boy for four years, not through choice. It was simply that living in the area I did and going to a Catholic school, you had to be one. Each week I watched the holy miracle, no not the wafer turning into the body of Christ but the hypnotic nap the entire congregation fell into as the priest started his sermon: the only opportunity he got to ad-lib as well. I even toyed with joining the priesthood, but alas I never got my calling which is a bit of a bummer as I look good in black and enjoy the company of young people. Of course when you state that you are a non-believer they try to convert you. Just tell them they have eternal life and that you, the atheist, have a relatively short one, so leave it be. Then they will quote from the good book, a book they base their lives on without even knowing who wrote it.

There are also the Gospels written by Matthew, Mark, Luke and John. Don't know their surnames but feel free to base your life on those works as well. Also the Gospels were written at least sixty years after the events took place; I don't even trust what journalists write the next day! Don't get me wrong, I firmly believe that Jesus existed but he was a prophet like many others whose lives have been exaggerated somewhat. For instance, where Jesus came from there weren't many white people but over the years, hey presto, he has become whiter than white just like new improved Jesus. Isn't that the part of the world where all the dope grows? In those days they tended to use what grew out of the ground (the

McDonalds was miles away apparently). Suffice to say there would have been a lot of stoned people talking crap.

'Hey Matthew, have a drag on this.'

'Wow man, the Red Sea just parted, put it in the book, early on, let's reel them in.'

The gospels were written so long after the events, there would have been huge scope for some wild reminiscing.

'Hey Mark, remember that time we ran out of wine at the wedding and Jesus saved the day with his home-brew kit.'

'Yeah, and remember you had that mad dinner party and we all got stoned and drunk and had those terrible hangovers.'

'Yeah, Jesus, he didn't get up for three days.'

Take me now, Lord.

Come with me into the thoughtful nothingness and remember, even if I'm wrong (I'm not one for dogma), surely if God is the good bloke he is supposed to be, he will forgive me.

'De-caf for me thanks, Cliff.'

# Lost Love

My stomach feels funny
It's either breakfast or love
both of which are needed
to make a good start to the day
My body feels the size
of a person spotted in the distance
It comprises water, nicotine, vomit,
tubing and little particles which ache
at various points.
And the future highlight being shopping
on the lost love aisle which only makes
room for baskets.
The colourful packaging of those ready
made non-compromising stomach-churning
Plastic spoilt-for-choice vegetarian frozen
snackettes
and we didn't love each other
but we helped each other forget
that life is shit
unfortunately I kept remembering
at the most inopportune moments
but when you see me smiling in the arms of what will
no doubt be connected to a beautiful face
you will know I am very alone.
Is it cold or is it just me.
All of a sudden I realize that the Beatles were terrible.
We can work it out. Indeed.

# The Great Outdoors

I moved to London over nine years ago and I have been steadily moving further and further away from the centre ever since. I'm presently located at N8; middle age should see me in Watford. When I first arrived, I was taken in by the excitement of Leicester Square. I was so impressed by the bright lights that I didn't see the parking meter in front of me which I proceeded to smash into. These days I rarely visit the centre, in fact, I rarely leave my house. This is for two reasons, one being the cost of housing – the more you stay in, the better value for money you get. Secondly, watching *Eastenders* made me too frightened to go out, in case I encounter any of them. I only know one proper Londoner. His name is Alfie and he's a diamond geezer, sorted, heart-of-gold kind of bloke. He's a wheeler-dealer, Frank Stubbs with facial hair, and this weekend he made me laugh out loud. Driving through London, a guy stopped us and asked for three pence.

'What do you want it for?' Alfie said.

'Me mate wants to buy a sandwich.'

Alfie retorted, 'Here's sixpence, get us one as well.'

Alfie was driving me to the Madness gig at Finsbury Park. London's motorists might well know him. Think of those times when you are driving carefully and there's a nutter behind you, beeping his horn and shouting at you for no apparent reason. That's Alfie. At the concert itself, he seems to know everybody, including the band. It's odd to see the band, these down-to-earth blokes, pottering away while in a few minutes' time, they will play to over forty thousand people. I don't like meeting celebrities because I never have anything to say to them and usually end up just staring at them until I'm asked to leave. I tell Suggs how much I like all their hits and in actual fact the only one I've never liked is 'Driving in my Car'. I leave them to get ready while I soak in the atmosphere, which is a euphemism for steadily getting more drunk. In the middle of my haze, I was sure Suggs had mentioned my name on stage. I asked a friend and he said, 'Don't be stupid', but it turned out he dedicated 'Driving in my Car' to me.

I have no recollection of going to bed, which is always a worry, the more so in London with the frequency of murders –

I wouldn't have an alibi. I awake in the morning cursing not having drunk that pint of water before going to bed and realizing that I'm supposed to be playing celebrity football against Crystal Palace. When somebody rings up and asks, 'Do you play football?' I usually say yes, momentarily forgetting that I have no football skills to speak of. I played a charity match a month ago and I was rubbish. I disguised this rather well by running around the pitch a lot. Spectators think I am getting into useful positions when in fact I am just trying to avoid the ball completely.

Unfortunately, you can't do this against a professional team. On my side, we had Dave 'Kid' Jensen, Steve 'Winger' Coppell, Graham 'Bread' Bickley, Steve '80s icon' Kember and Angus 'It's made from tea' Deayton. I was told to play up front, I nodded approvingly and went straight into the full-back position. The idea of missing open goal sitters in front of four thousand people didn't appeal. The team soon had me playing to my strengths by ignoring me. I can't shoot, pass, head or even spit properly. I tried but ended up with a dribble hanging out of my mouth. For some unknown reason, I'm not bad at tackling. I just stand there and, once they attack, I kind of run into them. We lost 5–3 and I was out of breath for the next three weeks. Of course the second I got home, my knee started pounding and I had to ask a friend if she'd play nurse as I couldn't move. She did a great job but kept complaining about the cut-backs, long hours and dowdy uniform. I sit here now with my bandaged knee for company, contemplating another quiet night in. I just don't like going out in London, but as taxi drivers will always tell you, 'If you're tired of London, you're tired of life.' Maybe I'm just tired of taxi drivers.

# Nobody's Out to Get Me

It's that time of year when I rush back to the bosom of my family. Admittedly, I'm a bit old to be breast fed but that's the kind of emotion Christmas brings out in me. My parents' house in Dublin always seems like a safe haven, away from the cut and thrust of London's acceptable level of violence. I remember when we bought it, we parked the car outside and my two brothers and I ran into the house sussing out our sleeping arrangements. You had to be fit as there were only two bedrooms for the three of us. We all had to put forward our arguments to see who would be King Pin and get the room to himself. I won and got to share the top room with my older brother. This made me happy because I was paranoid about the Psychopath. I even made sure that he had the bed closest to the door. Suburban Dublin seemed crime-free. Twenty years on, expecting the don't-let-the-bed-bugs-bite soft speak from my parents as they tucked me up for the night, I was shocked to hear of the likelihood of being burgled in the same suburb in 1995.

You can always tell the pulse of a city by its cab drivers. On driving back from the airport, mine offered, 'There's a murder here every week now. How long are you over for?' 'The week-end.' 'Oh, you'll probably get away with a stabbin'.' That should be nothing to me, living in the city that never sleeps, thanks mainly to my continuing paranoia and my bin men's habit of revving up their truck just outside my house at 6 a.m. Again, I thank the Lord for not being one of this year's crime statistics.

Christmas has me more relaxed. Not with the day itself, the five minutes of excited unwrapping of presents followed by the twenty-three hours and fifty-five minutes of saying that television isn't as good as it used to be. Realistically, it is the one day of the year where we get to know what it's like to be in prison. Trapped in a room with people you have very little in common with, with no chance of escape. No wonder there are so many break-out attempts straight after the festive season. But the thing I like about Christmas is knowing that criminals will be on their holidays too. It can't be much fun for their kids opening their presents and trying to contain their disappointment while saying, 'Thanks Dad, another second-hand video, great.' But it must be said that they deserve this break more than most. The unsociable hours battling against the weather, the continual threat of prison, the depression that looms as they ransack houses they can never afford, and of course the possibility of coming across one of those have-a-go heroes. Maybe I have a romantic view of criminals. That is probably because they have left me untouched. This is odd as I am what could be termed an easy touch. Single wimp in relatively big house who is away a lot. (COME AND GET ME!) But that's classified information. From the outside they will think: swanky alarm and ferocious dog and if they have been stalking my house, they are going to start to wonder why I never leave it.

The people who lived here before me had been done over six times in as many years and we are talking big family, two dogs and an alarm. I wouldn't mind, but I've made every effort for this eventuality. I leave my crappy shiny possessions quite near the front door, you know the kind of thing, CDs you couldn't hope to get rid of, watches that don't work and ornaments your folks give you. Another thing I do to confuse them is I get one of those police blue and white tapes with a sign saying Area Cordoned Off and chalk a body outline on the floor. I have also taken down my drain pipe. The police say they are more likely to go to a house that has one. And one of my daily rituals regardless of being burgled is before leaving the house I dump the contents of every drawer on the floor.

I suppose my dog is a little off-putting for them – my dog who is more scared than me, my dog who when he hears a noise tries to get into bed with me. My main cause for concern is that the burglar is really a burglar stroke killer. I foolishly keep a hammer beside my bed – not to hit anyone with, more in case I get a compulsion to hang some pictures. I am not going to fight back. At my most powerful, I could possibly mutter something in a raised voice, but I am a realist and I somehow don't think the thief, on seeing a skinny bloke in his underpants brandishing a hammer while shaking like a leaf, is going to be too disturbed. Of course the statistics try to ease your discomfort with facts like: most thieves are fourteen years of age. Well, funnily enough, most fourteen-year-olds could beat me in a fight. I would imagine that is why they never get caught when all the police have to go on are those fictional descriptions given by the victim out of embarrassment. 'Yes officer, he was about seven feet tall, the biggest bloke I've ever seen, I didn't stand a chance.'

Nowadays I've got a basic rule if anyone breaks into my house. It's theirs while they are here, I'll pop out for a bit and start shopping for replacements if that's OK. I sometimes contemplate hiring a security guard, or even outing myself so I can have a big, hairy biker type in my bed every night. He'd lie on the side nearest the door, obviously. Maybe I'll be less frightened when it actually does happen. Or maybe I am not paranoid about being burgled at all. In actual fact, my deep-rooted anxiety is that they are just plain ignoring me. Maybe they are worried that if they do me over I will make them stay and chat and listen to the new Tindersticks album. It is starting to get to me of late. Every time I get home and see my stuff intact, I think, 'What's wrong with me?'

# Bring Us Back a Parrot

It's holiday time, your once-a-year chance to get away from it all – get up at your own pace, a light breakfast, lazing about reading a book, a long stroll, the odd glass of wine, dinner with friends. Sounds ideal, well, that pretty much sums up my day-to-day life. Where the hell am I supposed to go? Two weeks in Spain doing light office work! I haven't had much luck with holidays, and that's not including the emotionally blackmailed childhood trips to my grandparents' house in Cork. 'Come on, kids, this might be the last time you see them alive.' That certainly put us in the holiday spirit. The whole break was geared towards that last day – the teary goodbyes and the fixed grin as Grandad handed us our ten pence. It was always ten pence, he never took heed of the hints we gave of the spiralling rates of inflation. It was always the same ritual, he'd call us out to the garden and put the coin into our palm via sleight of hand. We'd say thank you as we desperately tried to feel crooked edges in the hope that it was a fifty.

The question remains: where to go? Turkey? – a possible kidnapping. Australia? – don't hitch. Majorca? – beaten up by beer boys. Florida? – escort from airport by gun-toting luggage collectors. Thailand? – eight years in prison if caught with Alka Seltzer. Switzerland? – being bored to death. The last holiday I took was in Cairo, where I came across the worst conman in history. His patter went something like this (feel free to do the accent): 'Hallo my friend, I buy you coffee, I'm a teacher, I can get you all the great books free. I will bring them to your hotel later, first give me a hundred pounds.' I actually gave him the equivalent of sixty pounds, as it was my last day and I would have ended up buying some tac with it anyway, and also I wanted him to have a tale to tell for the rest of his life. Before that it was Barcelona. We rented a car, which was stolen on the second day; the contents of the second car were stolen on the third day. We got out of that city before the chain reaction really set in. Car firms have this beautiful system of sticking their brand name all over the car – you might as well leave every window open. It's a no lose situation for the thief as they play off the tourists' xenophobia. You can't really go into the local police station – 'What did he look like?' 'It's hard to say, because you all look the same.' Of course you comfort yourself by doubling the loss while filling in your insurance claim. It's only when you get home you realize you didn't read the small print which states you're not covered because you didn't hop on one foot for ten seconds and drink raspberry juice from an elephant's tusk at the time of the theft.

The strange thing about our society is that we use the holiday as an excuse to get away from the people we surround ourselves with and yet we all holiday in the exact same places. It's wonderful, you can now row with the neighbours all year round, only sometimes in a more interesting climate. There are in essence two types of holiday: sun seeking or culture hunt.

With the first it's basically days spent on the beach wondering whether it will be the fags or the sun that eventually gives you cancer, the odd bit of water sports (running into the sea to retrieve your ball), an evening meal in a shaded restaurant while all the time waiting for your holiday romance to begin. Women tend to go for Juan, the sensitive horse handler. You think he's a poet, but he's really just struggling with the English language. You dreamily remember him whispering, 'You are a mountain of beauty, a river of strength.' What he was trying to say was, 'You sweat a lot for a fat bird.' Men tend to fall for the bar waitress who wears too much make-up. The man isn't thinking about sex, it's the romantic notion of 'I can take you away from all this.' Without noticing that she's having fun in a sunny climate and what you are offering is a mundane life in front of the telly watching soaps. The reality of the situation is that Juan goes out with the waitress and they're having a laugh at your expense.

Day one is usually filled with the fatigue of having to turn to your travelling companions every five minutes to say, 'This is great, isn't it?' Day two – writing out postcards. Day three – finding post office. Day four – avoiding couple from Doncaster who think that because you speak the same language you've bonded. Day five – feeling hard done by, you go in search of the spot where the brochure pictures were taken from. Day six – reminiscing about the first five days. Last day – looking for couple from Doncaster because you're bored and they seem the best of a bad bunch.

The cultural holiday is spent roaming museums, art galleries and old-style architecture, while all the time secretly trying to locate the Irish bar, where you're determined to fall in love with the waitress. The only reason you go on a cultural holiday is so that on social occasions you can say you've been there. It's odd how some people can go away for a week, yet it takes them at least two to tell you all about it. The first-time holidayers are the worst: no matter where they go they always come back expressing this wish to live there. To me the pure joy of holidays is returning home, checking your phone messages, opening your post and disposing of the milk you forgot to throw out. The first thing to do is to ring up your travelling companion to try and patch up your differences. So where to go? The dictionary definition of holiday states: a season of idleness and recreation. I've booked myself on to the Crystal Palace football team this year.

# Family Matters

# Lover

'GLR 20, 20 travel: Crouch End Hill is closed due to a water-main being repaired. The whole area is congested with long tail-backs in all directions.'

'You don't say,' Peter replied to the radio as he sat in the middle of it all watching lights turning green to no effect. The rain was endless, further damaging the car which had decided to have a lie-in this morning anyway. He was going to be late for work, and what annoyed him more was that he knew he would be out of sync for the rest of the day: late lunch, late finish, he would have to forsake his recharging period, the snoozy lie down in front of the television, and instead rush out for his night of recreation. He wasn't used to dating, but it made sense with Maria. He felt he was almost in love with her, as near as he was ever going to get without a referee being called for. The two of them were the unmotivated indoor types, but brought together they became outgoing, they actually enjoyed doing things and didn't journey out just to make use of London's amenities. Tonight was her choice: Tapas bar, French film and decaffeinated discussion in an Italian café. She was very European in her way.

The lights turned green again as slugs overtook him, and now some crass Country and Western tune spilled out its heartache, the kind truckers in big hats fight over. He switched the dial, hoping to hear out-and-out aggression. 'Johnny Cougar fucking Melancamp.' He fumbled on the floor for tapes, blindly pushing aside dented cans and crisp packets. He grabbed the first tape to come within reach, caked in mud and grass, and without looking, popped it on. He rewound the tape, waiting for the surprise that destiny would bring him. He got off on the opening bars until he realized it was Deacon Blue. He ejected it, surmising he must have been in a fantastic mood the day he bought it. No music, just the silence of rain, horns, police sirens and temples booming. He tried the radio again. Every station played the same records only in a different rotation. He turned it off and decided to listen to the pounding bass from the flash nasty car nearby which his hangover was dancing to. This morning he had a foot hangover, the socks were sweaty, and a throbbing pain in the back of his leg took hold of his concentration. Last night was a boozy haze in the presence of his in-laws; although he was well over his limit, his nerves had kept him sober.

He had made it to the lights. To his left was the eyesore named Budgens, the non-league supermarket with no hope of promotion. He watched people running in the rain, sniggering at the fact that they believed going faster was somehow going to keep them drier. Others used the rain as an excuse to speed past the vendor selling *The Big Issue*. Peter noted the vendor was better dressed than him and couldn't help but smile at his soaked dog, ever faithful to its owner, but knowing he had been given a bum deal. The rain stopped and Noah was over-joyed.

Everybody slowed down half a pace and a rainbow appeared to his right, landing in Lloyds Bank. So that's where the pot of gold is. A beep, a jump and he was on his way. Things were looking up as he secured a parking space. A double yellow hidden from harm's way. He was an hour late. Gazing into the rear-view mirror he practised his apology and was annoyed he looked so pristine. He wanted to come across as he should, like one who had made every effort to get there on time. He took a moment to dishevel himself.

'Sorry, boss, burst water . . .'

'Peter.' He knew he was in trouble. 'You're fired.'

No pause for emotion: 'There's a week's wages.' Being human: 'I'm willing to write you a reference.' Logic prevailed. 'I've had complaints, no it's not the first, maybe you are not cut out for landscaping, you haven't the patience.' Compassion, then boss speak: 'It's over, you're giving the firm a bad name. There's a recession on. I can't afford a bad reputation. To be honest with you . . .' – killer blow – 'you are a liability.' Stunned groan followed by 'Thanks alot.' 'And bring all the equipment back by the end of the week.'

Peter was fuming. He walked to the door and slammed it in a futile response. The sun was shining on the land of unemployment. He practically bumped into one of the new green-shirted fascists who was administrating a parking ticket on his windscreen.

'What are you doing? I work here,' Peter lied. Forcing all his personality into the situation, the warden replied, 'Double yellow.' Peter ripped the ticket to shreds, his enemy started to write another. Peter was inconsolable, his legs started to wobble, his heart was thumping and his head was weightless. He was either going to faint or hit the guy. He had to act quickly, any thought process and no action would be taken. Rashness followed by history. He walked away, his bloodied hand shaking. The warden was grounded and his shirt would need one of those new improved washing powders, possibly two spins.

# Daughter

Maria was sixteen when she fell in love, not with something as tangible as another human being but with the idea of love itself. The second she saw Glenn Close and John Malkovich in *Dangerous Liaisons*, she knew it was possible. She also knew it was just a movie but it worked for her. She had never been taken in by the soppy pap that forced the last generation into the divorce courts. She was an only child, a souvenir of her parents' flirtations. Her over-protective father would always see her as just a child. Her teenage years had seen her bubble-wrapped into all the activities a wealthy family could afford, the memories kept in the Camcorder room. Her life had been mapped out by the supposed highlights of her future. No chance to daydream, very little lack of sleep. Her only worries were of the Brady Bunch variety. The only thing that made her stand out from the other girls in the boarding school was her total break-down, which left her hospitalized for six months, stress was blamed as a way of keeping individuals blameless. Of course to the outside world, she was never the same again and they were right: she had not changed, but their attitude towards her had. At least handicapped people were patronized on sight. Her parents, confused that health couldn't be bought, rushed out and got the best kid gloves money could buy. Maria didn't want to rebel against her parents. She loved them quietly; it was more their way of life that troubled her, the pretence of their existence, their lack of problems. She would never know her parents. Chit-chats didn't cover the basics. She was sure they had things to say, and at their funerals peers would tell of their personalities. They lazily loved each other, habits had merged, they were a single entity, dispassionate but pure, unhappy with their unlot. The romance had eroded and been replaced by her. She found this hard to handle and was soon hidden away in a one-bedroomed flat in Muswell Hill. She knew little of the area, but the estate agent personalized his estate agent speak with smiling references to Dennis Nielson's chatty murders. There was no doubting it was a beautiful house. Unfortunately, it was now four shabby flats, cheap conversions meant creaky floors, thin walls and kitch-enettes. She moved in with the minimum of fuss and furniture and was determined to be neither a borrower nor a lender of sugar.

Having severed links with the past, she didn't want them to be replaced with similar types. The nightmare of sharing your life with parents your own age was never far from her mind. She busied herself doing light duties in a small feminist publishing firm.

Without being conscious of it, she soon fell into the trap of a strictly time-tabled life. She would flick through the listings magazine *Time Out* to see what was happening. She had no interest in going out to any of these places, but it was a comfort to know it was all out there. She didn't even like the magazine but bought it out of habit. She skipped all the articles, as she had the impression they were writen by people while eating sandwiches.

A loveless existence was becoming her norm. She knew a life without love was an empty one, so she settled for a charitable one, spending half a day at a distressed dog unit. Having the same routine every day was a comfort, even though many of the things she did were not enjoyed, she was rarely aware of it. Sometimes as she sat in front of the television eating Rice Crispies, it would suddenly dawn on her that she hated her sofa, the TV programme and had always despised noisy food. Of course she would forget this next time she was out shopping as she was summoned to the usual shelves of the supermarket by lack of an inner voice. A staple diet for a stable person.

Nothing could really change as she had become one in the queue of those who do until the don'ts become the only option. In this case a car crash. The impact of the collision changing her life forever. Minor injuries, a shouting match and love at first sight. She even took him to meet her parents, who went beyond polite as they tried to hide the 'he's not exactly what we had in mind darling' look on their faces. They saw him as a jobless layabout with a seedy past; she saw him as free spirit, fighting against type. He considered himself as a bit of both. To others they appeared like brother and sister, there for each other without any of the signposted showing of love. The free spirit wasn't one for public displays of affection. The relationship had to work, for as time slowed there was nothing else, a danger they never deliberated on. The fusion between the two became their sole reason for existence, not so much the world revolving around them, more being revolted by the world. A healthy cynicism had been overtaken by a fatigued one, the kind that comes about by being slightly left of Mao. The apathy of knowledge meant that reading the right books was as far as their revolution would go. Anyway, they liked their little comforts. They were becoming concentrated orange juice socialists, apathetic only to apathetic people.

At work, the only place she could vent their carefully laid-out spleen, courtesy of eerie silences, her colleagues laughed at her. Being aware of social etiquette, they did this behind her back. The tattiness of her clothes was the prime target for their jokes, but soon they became vicious. They were frightened and jealous of her. They hated her self-absorption, her lack of ambition, the way she could never be infiltrated. Her depth was seen as idleness, for she would wear a dazed expression from nine to quarter past five, her face only coming to life as her frontdoor closed. The rest of the assembly line wished for such love affairs. The only way they could deal with it was to circle and pick at it.

Soon they were both working. She didn't like this. Him being contaminated by others and coming home to have his own news to talk about. This is when she started fighting with him. Her heart was in the right place, but sadly both their spaces were being violated. The only way to express this hint of loss was to see how far she could take it, how much he would take. In analysis, years later, she would blame her parents, the doctor's nod, proof of her argument. A new pattern evolved. She would give him a hard time, he would take it out on others, they survived in their grey bliss, until again the don'ts became the only option. This time a phone call. He was accused of murder. She was put on heavy medication.

# Mother

'Capital Gold prize bonanza. We have Sam Davies on the line. Who do you think the voice belongs to, my darling?'

'Is it Billy Idol?'

'Uh, nice try but you're . . . wrong. Sorry love, next caller.'

The wardrobe slid open with gentle fast ease. The dark aided by assembled beams of light offered a multitude of choice: dresses, shoes, hats. Valerie stared in at the various designer labels, little memories attached to each garment. She lost herself for a time but quickly snapped back into this colour-coded affair. Comfort, style and room temperature would all have to be taken into account. The problem being, she wasn't dressing for herself, more to make a composite picture at the party. Three dresses lay on the bed muscling for attention, each trying to outshine the others as if they had made it to the finals of some pageant. Valerie sat by the mirror, eyeing them through the reflection as she started the beautification session, a laboured event considering she didn't want to go. A function of fixed grins loosened by Martinis, snacks and sound-bites. The evening would consist of faintly concerned chin-wags, discreet mutterings of gossip and the odd stony silence as news of her daughter's collapse broke. In its time, this too would become talked about until somebody else's angst toppled it. She would know practically every woman there, thrown together not by friendship but by virtue of being married to a shithead. This wasn't an indictment of their spouses' personalities, more to do with the fact that they worked in the highly profitable business of waste disposal.

On one such occasion, Valerie had bonded with the openly contemptuous Judith Bennett. They had met and clicked and started to socialize outside of the circle. It was a whirlwind friendship. One minute they weren't aware of each other's existence; the next, they were bosom pals. They spent this spell laying out layable secrets in quick-fire succession, always giddy with excitement, too long in the tooth to set down proper foundations, knowing their relationship wouldn't last. The earthquake came on the night Valerie stayed over to find Judith touching parts of her body her husband couldn't even name. It is safe to say she was turned on. Luckily she realized it wasn't in a sexual way but by the idea of something new happening. Nothing was ever said, and they drifted as quickly as they had met. It wasn't that she didn't want to talk about it, but had trouble coming to terms with the terrible sadness she felt at one person trying to force her sexuality upon another.

There was nothing like sex to make humans show their pathetic side and anyway, she took on her quota of the blame for being so naive to Judith's lust. She was still of the mind that not everything was necessarily motivated by sex, even though every experience had taught her otherwise.

The only fun ahead for her tonight was in guessing who her husband was having an affair with at this instant. She could always tell. It would be the woman he dare not look at on arrival, be curt to in company and find himself sitting beside as the night started swinging, but always remembering to be with a bunch of men as the canapé plates became ash trays. The stupid bastard had settled into a system: a few late nights at work, a business trip followed by an inordinate amount of time spent at home. He thought he had covered his tracks, conning his doting wife, the wife whose looks, he felt, had faded while he got away with the distinguished look.

The funny thing was, she was happy with the scenario. During his little rash skirmishes, the atmosphere at home was much more relaxed, his guilt trips placated the house and she was glad somebody else was on sex duty. There was the worry that there would come a time when he considered one of his binges as a possible dream future. The excitement of a delayed nothing new seen through rose-patterned short skirts, weighing the balance in the other woman's favour. A cosy flat to share their *déjà vus* in. She didn't feel oppressed, she understood the need to fill the void, she just couldn't go through with it herself: the perfumed liaisons, dark corners of obscure restaurants, the heady impulsiveness, the long bubble baths, the drifty dreaminess, all that effort purely to let the animal out of the cage for a moment. She was content to live this through her husband. She pictured him talking nonsense as his loins went into overdrive.

'You see the problem is, my wife understands me too much and I need to escape that on occasion.'

He knew that she was aware, but again no information was passed. Those silences eventually sharing the silences of old age, regret speaking loudest. Her knowledge gave her strength, a strength her husband despised. If they were invited on to the Oprah Winfrey show, she would be of the opinion that his continual womanizing was his way of proving her right.

She chose a green off-the-shoulder number, nothing too revealing but it was nice to let him see what he was missing once in a blue moon. Crow's-feet were powdered, but she wasn't one for living in fear of losing her looks.

She was more frightened of finding herself walking in parks in 90 degrees heat, sniffling with a constant cold, wearing a long overcoat, carrying two plastic bags full of assorted necessities. The only fate worse was being accompanied by an equally decrepit partner whose sole purpose in life was to feed the ducks.

Before she closed the wardrobe, she peeked a look at her wedding dress, once pure white, now sour cream. A happy day, butterflies in her stomach enhanced the moment: 'I do'. He was insane with love, the kind that can't possibly last but which the other partner grows accustomed to. A love that is permanently chiselled away at until you come to the core of being comfortable with each other.

She loved him, always would, but never felt in love with him. This is why she felt this stage he was going through wasn't difficult to handle, but she also realized that this was her thought for now; a conflicting one would be along at any moment, possibly three; she knew she would lose out in the end. Her husband walked in.

'I have to go away on business next week.'

She was sure there were other pleasantries but she didn't take them in. She sneaked out of her green dress and replaced it with a less revealing one – black, to match her gloom.

# Father

The company Flush Ltd had expanded beyond reason. A frightful amount of money had gone into four bank accounts, and two of the men responsible sat ten feet apart on either side of a huge mahogany table: Frank Fenton and Jerry Burns, friends from college, faced each other now as successful business partners. The pair were from the right side of town, the side where good luck is taken for granted. They were perfect together, Frank with his business head and Jerry with his sporty personality. Both were married, Frank with one child, Jerry, the athlete, bearing four. The more money they made, the further apart they would sit. They seemed to have the Midas touch. What had been a joke in a youthful marijuana haze now made the expression 'living beyond one's means' a redundant one.

'What's up?' Jerry said, in a 'we've known each other for ages, let's get straight to the point' kind of way.

Frank monotoned, 'Things couldn't be better. Three new long-term contracts, the new software is way ahead of the competition and the government grant for the Birmingham branch makes it a no lose situation. Oh, and by the way, I love you.' A sigh.

'What's up?' sternly.

'Huh?'

'Come on, I've known you for twelve years, I've never seen you like this. You're preoccupied, what's on your mind?'

'It's a blank, I don't know what you are talking about.'

'I think you do. You are putting in very irregular hours. Are you having problems at home?'

Frank replied with his eyebrows.

'If I didn't know you better, I'd say you were on the verge of a nervous breakdown.'

'Yeah, it runs in the family.'

'I'm sorry, I didn't think.'

'It's OK . . .' perking up a bit, 'Do you ever think life is passing you by?'

Jerry, standing, gesticulating, 'What are you talking about? You've got it all.'

'Have I?'

'Take a break.'

Frank mumbles, 'Yeah, have a Kit Kat.'

'I don't like this, Frank.'

Frank ambled over to the window, looked out moodily, as if in a movie. 'Have you got any friends?'

'You're my friend.'

'Am I?'

'Because you're a friend, I can take that.'

'That's big of you.'

'And that.'

Frank gathering momentum: 'What have you done in your life?'

'Look around you.'

'We're cardboard cut-outs, aren't we?'

'What are you trying to say?'

'You can't ignore what you've become.' A sigh.

'Get real.'

'*That*'s what I'm doing.'

'You're making me nervous.'

'Live a little.'

'Frank, just leave, okay,' summoning up his senior partner authority, but not meaning it all the same.

'What are you frightened of?' Frank asked, not budging.

'What are *you* frightened of?'

'You don't answer a question by repeating a question, college boy.'

'Look, don't take your shit out on me.'

'I thought it was all part of our service,' said Frank, killing the tension. He sits down then stands up again quickly.

'Where are you going?'

'To get some fresh air.'

'This room is air conditioned.'

'Maybe that's the problem.'

'I don't get it, I just don't get it. These fucking riddles.'

'I'm going away for a while. Don't let anyone near my computer.' He becomes a dot on Jerry's horizon.

Jerry goes to the intercom. 'Miss Gordon, bring me up all Mr Fenton's floppy disks.'

He didn't think he was intruding. Frank obviously wanted him to see it, otherwise he wouldn't have mentioned it. Frank could do wonders with a computer. He could get into any system with perseverance. He had used it unfairly, dare it be said criminally, at the company's instruction in the early days. This was before computer crime had even been given a name. When Jerry saw what was in front of him, his chest tightened and he was in two minds whether or not to call the police, but for the time being settled on turning the air conditioning up a notch.

# Eleven Angry Men and One Bored One

'All rise.' Julian had just sat down. The hardest task today was keeping in the snigger caused by the outdated pomposity of the wigs around the court. Julian was on jury service for a grim murder in grim London, in from the grim sunshine, he prayed that the grim reaper would come and take him away.

The court clerk announced, 'We are here to pass judgement on the case of the Queen versus Peter Boland . . .

Julian wished he'd brought a Walkman.

*Mama, just killed a man.*

'. . . who is charged with the murder of one Graham Silgardo, for on the tenth day of November 1994, he unlawfully killed . . .'

Julian muttered, 'like you can lawfully kill someone'.

'. . . the aforementioned Graham Silgardo with malice aforethought. The court calls upon the prosecution to make his opening speech.' This could go on for fucking ages, thought Julian. He had tried his darndest to get out of it, arriving in combat trousers, greased hair pulled back into a ponytail, two days' facial growth, but instead was deemed part of what could be called a 'good cross-section' and was now trapped with another eleven people of the sort he had spent most of his life trying to avoid.

The jury listened to various authoritarian figures throwing facts at them which they were to disassemble in their own little designated room. Julian thought Peter had committed the crime but felt like pleading for his innocence, purely to get back at the head juror, whose uneducated slow thud of thought was coming from too many readings of the Old Testament.

*Galileo, Galileo, Galileo let him go, Beelzebub has a devil put aside for me . . .*

He didn't know which was worse, head honcho or the excitable business man who had obviously missed his vocation as Morse, as he left no stone unturned in his quest for absolute truth.

'Yeah, yeah, OK on the surface, it looks like a sure thing but isn't it just possible that he was set up? Several people knew his movements, somebody who knew him . . . and what about the phone call? Somebody actually called the council to let them know about the car on the double yellow line . . .'

Yeah, and I suppose the FBI killed Kennedy, Julian didn't bother to wise crack.

'. . . Anyone could have called. People do get annoyed.'

'What are you talking about? He's actually admitted to manslaughter. It's just a matter of how many years we put the thug away for.'

*Carry on, carry on, nothing really matters.*

Julian moved towards the window. The others, thinking he was deep in thought, looked to him, but in fact he just wanted to fart. The token black member spoke up. 'I just don't get it. You don't just beat someone to a pulp because you get a parking ticket.' The Moses of the group went into full flight. 'He has a history of violence in his family.'

*Too late, my time has come, sends shivers down my spine, body's aching all the time.*

Julian spoke for the first time. 'His family, maybe, but not him. Jesus, I wouldn't like my family's shit dropped at my door.' They dismissed his coarseness out of hand.

They were summoned back to court to listen to the defence. Julian feared for Peter's future. The eleven angry men perked up, feeling very pleased with themselves, wearing stern, all-knowing, self-congratulatory smiles. Julian knew Peter was doomed. Christ, he was sure one of them had whistled on the way back to the court.

*We are the champions, my friends.*

Although they were only half-way through the case, Julian

sensed the inevitable. Much like in the Eurovision Song Contest when, after only six countries have voted, you just know Ireland are going to win.

# Defenders of Truth

The defence and prosecution barristers sat at their usual table in the corner of the restaurant obscured by the cloakroom where customers left their coats and car stereos. The formality of ordering pizzas over with, they jokily mocked each other's court gestures. This competitive streak kept them hungry.

'Ah, come on, Rupert, there's nothing to get my teeth into here. There's no skill called for. You killed off any chance of plea bargaining by bringing up that dodgy rape case. That was below the belt.'

'Just doing my job, Gerald. Anyway, you got it struck off the record.'

'Yeah, like the jury is going to forget that. It was nasty.'

'True . . . he's going down anyway . . . what do you think he'll get?'

'If we're very lucky, eight for manslaughter with a little diminished responsibility thrown in.'

'Dream on. The victim didn't even throw a punch.'

'Don't finish on that.'

'Let's face it, he's fucked.'

'Let's eat.'

The waitress bounced over. She knew them well enough to allow them to flirt with her.

'When are you going to let me take you away from all of this?' Rupert proposed.

'You're a married man,' put curtly.

'Yeah, I know, I meant with me and my wife.' Smiles all round.

'Eat your food.' She peppered and Parmesaned and was on her way.

'I can't stop looking at tits in this weather,' Gerald, baring his soul.

'I know what you mean. I nearly lost it in court looking at Rachel's profile.'

'You were just getting off on her outfit,' offered Gerald, thinking there was enough of a junction to start eating.

'Naw, it's just the prim and proper way she carries herself.'

'It's a classic taking her from behind scenario,' Gerald's penis spoke.

Water was sipped, grease was licked, Gerald's head moved nearer to the table.

'I bet she's a devil in bed.'

'A screamer,' Rupert confessed a tad too quickly.

'You haven't, have you?'

'A long time ago.'

Rupert extended, taking too much pizza into his mouth, giving Gerald enough time to digest the information.

'Well?'

'To tell you the truth, it was a bit off-putting.'

'How?'

Looking around, out of habit, Rupert lowered his voice. 'I thought she was taking the piss. OTT – you know what I mean. I ended up groaning along.' Their eyes became child-like. They moved closer as Gerald was taken aback. 'This got her going even more. Jesus, she was intense, all big eyes and instructions. Then, and I'm not joking, she started moaning, 'Put it in me now, Daddy?''

'Fuck off.'

'I did. After that, I got a puncture and couldn't get out of there fast enough.'

Then, stopping Gerald's exasperation, he continued, 'To make matters worse, she had these two cats who were watching the sorry state of affairs.'

Gerald asked hundreds of questions, taking in the information again and again, in various different forms, only stopping when every last detail had been squeezed out. Content, he said, 'I'll never be able to look her straight in the face again.'

'How do you think I feel?'

'Has she ever said anything?'

'What do you think?'

'Do you fancy a pudding?'

'No, I'll be too stodgy for the afternoon. I don't want to start repeating during the summing-up.'

'You've lost it anyway,' Gerald said, bringing the conversation back to business.

'I was hoping that story might cause a little concentration lapse.'

'What? It was bullshit?'

'I only wish.'

'Hey, do you fancy doing one of our bets?' excited.

'What's the subject?' more excited.

'Rachel, of course. Come on, ten pounds to see if we can refer to her in the summing-up.'

'OK.' They shook hands.

'What are you going to say?' Gerald wondered.

'I've got it,' Rupert started smiling. 'I'll say it was just a temper which went too far. It wasn't premeditated. He wasn't some action hero, a superman or a catwoman, there to hit a few choice-chops.'

'Excellent, I won't be able to keep a straight face.'

'What about you?'

'I think I'll go for the murder is murder and you only have to think of the victim, catching his last breath, his thoughts with his loved ones, screaming out in terror for his mummy and daddy.'

'You wouldn't!'

'Watch me.'

'Do you think she'll twig?'

'Not a chance.'

The waitress left the bill.

'Can her skirt get any smaller?' Gerald jeered, emitting an animal noise. 'Leave a big tip, Rupert.'

# Murderer

'A man consumed by passion is a danger to himself. A man with no passion is a danger to others.' This passage haunted Frank. It came from an airport thriller which he had bought at a railway station, purely for the escapism. It surprised him that it hadn't washed over him as the rest of the book had. His marriage wasn't a sham, but at its best, it was convenient. His daughter he loved and despised in equal measures. He was too clever for his job and, in total, had outgrown his life. An overhaul would be too much effort; a new hobby, not enough. He had started to hurt the ones he loved as an exercise in how low he could go. In essence, he was rejecting what he had always longed for. His muddled state of tedium left him continually blunt. He started drinking heavily but realized he couldn't pull it off. The odd liaison filled him full of inadequacy. The only thing that kept him going was the falsehood of memory and the horror of the future.

One Sunday morning, the papers had annoyed him. The joy of the reflecting hour was gone. His wife was a robot and his daughter was in love with a despicable character. He didn't know if it was the rising statistic of unsolved murders or the security check he did on Peter Boland which made him take such drastic measures. His only objective in life became to destroy this man's. He undertook his task with an enthusiasm he had not felt since starting up his business. He was still amazed that people never knew how much information could be obtained about them via a computer, and even more so, how easily it could be altered. As a prank he once changed his senior partner's credit rating on the day they were due to go out for an expensive dinner with an important client. His partner Jerry was renowned for his rudeness to waiters, which made it all the sweeter surveying his red face as all his cards were refused. Watching the head waiter cut them in half at the request of American Express was probably the last time Frank laughed out loud.

The joy of destroying something lay in building it up first, a common media ploy. He needed to know Peter's whereabouts. He found he had been unemployed most of his life. A job was called for. One he would enjoy, too. There's nothing like a false sense of security. Frank plumped for gardening. Peter created a good impression by all accounts and became a better person for it. Frank kept tabs on him daily. His one flaw was with his punctuality. At the garden centre they saw him as an affable, hard-working type. They weren't to know he had lost three previous jobs for fighting. Once a pattern was developing, Frank decided it was time to play God with him. He sent his real records, including one Peter Boland's acquittal from a rape charge, to the workplace. This was dominoed by a dismissal and Frank's phone call to the local parking authority.

Looking back on it, Frank had lost all rhyme to his reasoning but couldn't stop. The challenge was there. Of course he didn't want to see his daughter suffer, but suspected this would surely tip her over the edge again. Nor did he think about the consequences of things going wrong. With murder, you can't rely solely on computer skills. Bytes never left anything to chance. Frank started questioning his decisions. The apparent joy of murder was surely being able to tell others about it. Maybe he was doing just enough to ensure he got caught. Then there was also the possibility that he might feel remorse and be plagued by guilt for eternity. Or, worse still, get so excited by the deed that he would kill again. And to think his wife thought he was pre-occupied by other women.

It was when contemplating the thought of being charged with murder that the big change of heart came. The day was picked. He was away on business in Birmingham, as the records would show. The garden centre was sent records of Peter's criminal past, first class. A drinking session the night before left him groggy. A loose wire stalled his car. Frank watched him get into the office that morning, an hour late. Bingo! he rang the local parking authority. As Peter fumed out, he had a left-eyed view of the attack, and the sight of this pure naked aggression, coupled with the thought of his daughter being touched by him, justified his intent. He observed Peter driving off and hated him. A crowd started to acknowledge the event – he had to work fast. He rushed over and, under the pretence of helping the battered man with mouth to mouth, he suffocated him. There was no struggle. The crowd had gathered, blinking. Frank disappeared.

In a matter of days, Peter was under arrest, Frank's daughter in hospital, his wife near to Valium and his task achieved. It was peculiar then, that he still felt incomplete and actually felt emptier, with moments of outrageous regret. But, stranger still, he felt incapable of what he'd just done. He reckoned Peter would go down for manslaughter at the very least, his daughter would soon return to her state of the walking dead, and his wife would continue to have her emotions led by the soap operas. The Monday morning found him back at his real profession. Toying with the computer, he noticed one of the employees had died of a heart attack. As he arranged his pension, an idea struck him and within half an hour, the dead man was on the jury panel for Peter's case, brought to life by a heavily disguised Frank. He figured that out of fifteen candidates, he was guaranteed a place in court. It made him scared for those sorts in prison who insist they didn't do it.

# The Verdict

A light, tasteless grey meal churned around Peter's stomach. He hadn't been to the toilet all day. A sense of rage surrounded him as the two policemen led him back to the dock. He had been frightened to look into the faces of his judge and jury, but now that a verdict had been reached, he could stare them out, strangers who held his destiny, oddly familiar looking, they had jumped out at him in various nightmares, differently shaped faceless faces. His mind was spinning. He didn't want the geezer in the wig condemning him to a life of table-tennis. Think positive: male-bonding, acquiring a new skill, various drugs, fitness, an appreciation of soft porn photos, someone to watch early evening television with, the feeling of being wanted, early nights, books that wouldn't have been read, tall stories, cooked meals, free clothes, a job, a roof over his head and a chance to cut down on his smoking. He stood there with a grin on his face, much to the dismay of those around him. It was a fearful smile, one that had him so scared he lost control of his nervous system and had become unaware of his own postures. The recurring thought of how did it possibly happen, confused and belittled him.

The judge saw it as a straightforward case, emotions didn't come into it. Twenty years on the bench, he had mellowed in heart but not in sentencing. The jury, looking like a team, despised each other's morals. The family of the victim, seething in quiet despair, sat on uncomfortable benches on the balcony, focusing in on the back of the accused, mentally noting to hate that particular style of haircut hereafter. Quirky types made up the numbers, the ones not satisfied with the gore our television sets dispel upon us. The smells in the room, taken for granted by the regulars, swelled up inside the visitors' lungs, cutting up air vents with moist decay. The lost souls hovered above the room, refusing to leave even though their bodies were safely locked away. Sweat dried on all handles as windows tried to push themselves open.

'Have you come to a decision?'

The anxiety attack was revving up all its energy, ready to explode into his immune system, the need to pace only heightened by the unnerving way his legs refused to move. The head juror stood up. His suit fitted him too well. It didn't suit the occasion. Everything should be imperfect. The head juror was nervous with his responsibility. Frank's mind started to play tricks – maybe he would read out the wrong verdict. The pizza was repeating for the defence; the prosecution was hungry again and kept sneaking looks over at Rachel. The accused was soon in short trousers.

He was twelve again and being chastised for pinching apples; innocent maybe, but he knew this terror. He knew he couldn't walk away. His parents couldn't bail him out. All his sanity was draining away. He wanted to plead for his innocence, promising not to do it again, asking God for forgiveness. A simple apology wouldn't do. Then a leap and he thought of files and cakes and helicopters. Then he remembered his childhood hadn't been that great.

Frank wished he could turn back the clock or at the very least become an acquaintance of Doctor Who; availing of the Tardis he'd love to erase twenty odd years. He had made a mistake and had stupidly let emotions take him over. He also saw Peter's childlike qualities and couldn't help but see some of himself in the accused, not good traits but ones that made him feel better about himself. Frank felt dizzy. He covered his face with his clammy hands and tried to catch his breath. He needed comfort but his wife and daughter were elsewhere. 'Guilty' popped out. The family of the victim were as happy as they knew how to be. The court artist grabbed his pencils and rushed out, ready to draw the story. He'd done a pretty good job. He felt like showing Peter his likeness. The court emptied, identical people took their place. It was only an hour later that Peter dared ask how long his sentence was. He had been given thirty years. He had to sit down, he felt he was either going to faint or hit someone. As Peter collapsed, three million people around Britain were just settling down to watch *Countdown*. The sun shone, it was a Tuesday, it was 4.33 p.m.